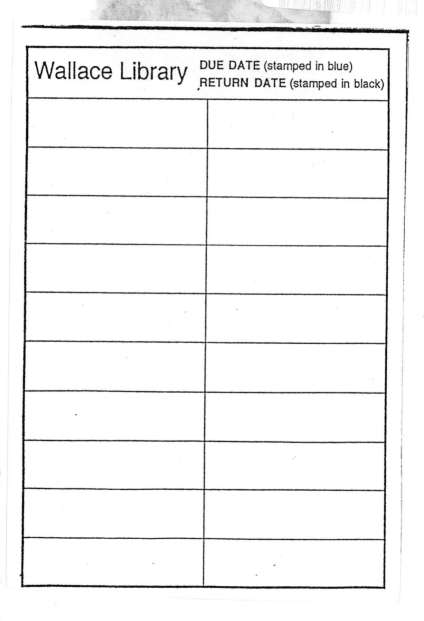

OUTLINES OF RUSSIAN CULTURE

Part III

Architecture Painting and Music

By

PAUL MILIUKOV

•

Edited by

MICHAEL KARPOVICH

•

Translated by

VALENTINE UGHET and ELEANOR DAVIS

A PERPETUA BOOK ∞

A. S. BARNES AND COMPANY, INC.
New York

CONTENTS

I

ARCHITECTURE

THOSE who have visited some of the great Gothic cathedrals in Europe during the celebration of high mass know from experience the artistic charm with which the Western church meets and surrounds the religious needs of the faithful. Rows of massive pillars, which appear bound together by clusters of slender columns, raise their graceful lines to the vaulted ceiling where they spread and interweave like the branches of gigantic palms. The entire space is submerged in a mysterious semi-darkness, which emphasizes the intricate pattern of the tall stained-glass windows. From somewhere the deep chords of an organ fill the air with solemn sounds; suddenly the sharper, more definite melody of a stringed orchestra strikes through these vibrant tones, then, after a moment of silence, the voice of a soloist is heard. One came here to look at famous monuments of art but, seeing in the pews the forms of fervent worshipers, and listening to the distant intoning of the priest accompanied by the rapid ringing of a bell, for a time one forgets that the surrounding walls are crowded with beautifully carved tombs and that in the niches of the numerous chancels are holy pictures, each representing a memorable event in the history of Christian painting. One forgets the purpose of the visit and involuntarily surrenders oneself to the pervading mood.

But the purpose of the student-tourist will not suffer from this spell, because it has brought him into the very focus of the medieval conception of the world, which fundamentally created Western art. The church was the laboratory in which art was fostered and where, even to a larger degree than literature, it reached its full development. Being anxious to retain within its fold the creations of the new period in art and, through their medium, to maintain its power over the soul of modern man, the church was willing to make broader concessions to new ideas in the field of art than to those in science and philosophy. Therefore only slowly and by degrees did the secular element in art replace the sacred.

Cimabue and Giotto, acclaimed by their contemporaries, departed from the symbolism and conventionality of the Byzantine style, although they both continued to adhere to religious themes. After them came the immediate precursors of Raphael and Raphael himself, who still avoided breaking away from religious subjects while instilling into them a purely secular feeling. The transition from sacred to the secular was equally gradual in music. Palestrina was the first to reform the traditional style of church music, after which new ideas were introduced by Bach, Handel, Haydn, and Mozart. Western religion yielded to the demands of a strong secular feeling, but it also retained for a long period the power of arousing the artist's inspiration and of supplying the substance for more and more great works of art. For a vital and organic development of religious art in the East no such conditions existed.

Nevertheless, Eastern and Western art had a common source; they had both been developed from the Hellenic art of the early Christian centuries which, with the help of technical means and methods inherited from the art of the classical world, was the first to solve the artistic problems of the new religion. Classical art was breathing its last and its end was quickened when early Christianity exacted from it the new and unusual task of replacing realism with mystical symbolism. Christianity had no need for the naturalism of classical art and could just as readily dispense with its technique, for Christians wanted their most abstract ideas represented by conventional signs of a more or less primitive nature. The chief task of early Christian art was the creation of a cycle of symbolic figures to represent these abstract ideas graphically without revealing their meaning to the uninitiated.

In the face of such a trend, realism in artistic representation was soon replaced by conventionality. Both the art of painting and of sculpture sank rapidly from the heights they had attained during the classical period, and only in the field of architecture did Christian art make steady progress. From its very inception architecture had had to solve independently the very difficult problem of creating a spacious Christian temple, a new form of building not as yet foreseen in the classical period. Christian art solved the problem brilliantly in a series of variations, each exceeding its predecessor in perfection. It first created a Christian basilica, well proportioned and covered with a roof supported on wooden beams; next a Byzantine church with a hemispherical dome; then the ogee-vaults and massive walls of a Romanesque church; and finally the very incarnation of architectural lightness and elegance—the Gothic cathedral with sharp, pointed arches and vaults, massive pillars, and walls of stone lace-work pierced with stained-glass windows, which lent to the edifice an ethereal appearance.

Architecture, having definitely established itself, was able to lend its support to sculpture. At first, for architectural purposes, the mere decoration of walls, and then for independent purposes as well, the artist began to imitate ancient sculptors and sought to attain their mastership in the modeling of human figures. This required a knowledge of natural science and the study of the human body; sculpture thus led Christian art towards direct representation, the path followed by classical but abandoned by medieval art. Having trained his eyes and hands to work upon tangible, rounded figures, the artist could not avoid introducing life-like forms into painting. Just as progress in architecture had led to the development of sculpture, so did sculpture lead the art of drawing away from its medieval primitiveness. In accepting the imitation of life and reality as their aim, both the figurative arts gradually overstepped their original boundaries. If at the beginning direct representation was only the means of producing a religious impression, subsequently to be true to nature became an aim in itself, while art ceased to pursue any religious design and became secular. Unhampered by outside interference, Western art very gradually and unwittingly effected the complete transition from a religious inspiration to the admiration of nature and life. Therefore there was no forced interruption between Christian and profane, ecclesiastic and secularized art; one naturally was conceived by the other.

But in Russia and the Orthodox East the fate of Christian art was quite different. In Russia, as in the West, it was introduced with the conversion, yet we must not forget that in each case the event coincided with an absolutely different moment in the history of early Christian art. Germanic Europe was converted in the sixth and seventh centuries A. D., when early Christian art was passing through its first brilliant era. The preparatory period (IV–VI centuries) had just ended, and the artist had scarcely had time to master the themes provided by the new religion. These new subjects were represented by forms adopted from classical art, so that Christian art of the early days appeared to be only its sequel. While the artist never considered repudiating the artistic types and methods of classical technique, he retained the independence he acquired during the first efforts necessary to represent Christian subjects. In those days the various methods for the solution of identical artistic problems had not as yet been coördinated. The fact that Christian art had no established types provided a free and wide scope to the imagination and individual taste of the artist. Thus, abounding in vitality, Christian art passed from the East into the hands of Western artists, and it was only the victory of Germanic barbarism over ancient civilization that brought it for several centuries to a dormant state. During the twelfth century this temporary inertia, however, came to an end, and life and movement once again pervaded the Christian art of Western Europe.

Conditions were different in Russia. When, towards the end of the tenth century, the new faith was accepted by the Russians, early Christian art was already definitely Byzantine. Its period of free creative activity was terminated; all themes had been developed and all types permanently established. In observance of the Commandment "Thou shalt not worship false gods and idols" and also to avoid the censure of the iconoclasts, the Seventh Ecumenical Council (787) forbade the worshiping of graven images. Moreover, Epiphanius, one of its members, expressed the opinion that in painting icons artists should not have unlimited

ARCHITECTURE

freedom, because "it is not the invention of the painter that creates the picture but an inviolable law and tradition of the Orthodox church. It is not the painter but the holy fathers who have to invent and dictate. To them manifestly belongs the composition, to the painter only the execution." True, the Council in its decisions did not include this opinion, but it characterizes nevertheless the spirit of Byzantine art. Towards the end of the ninth and the beginning of the tenth centuries the decoration of cruciform churches assumed an almost canonical significance; the Pantocrator was placed in the dome, the Holy Virgin in the apse, icons commemorating holidays in the central part of the church, and the Last Judgment on the wall facing the sanctuary. All icons were painted in a strictly established form. "Divine Grace should be ever present in imagery as in Scriptures," Simeon of Thessalonica wrote in his *Dialogue against Heretics*.

This, however, does not mean that during its entire length of history Byzantine art manifested no inner stir or progress. Early opinion as to the complete immobility of Byzantine art has been definitely disproved in the brilliant research works of Millet, Diehl, and Dalton, and their Russian colleagues, N. P. Kondakov, Muratov, and others. Following upon its first flourishing period Byzantine art, on the contrary, had two other "golden ages," one during the era of the Comneni (IX–X centuries) and the other during that of the Paleologi (XIII–XIV centuries).

Russia was the last to enter the Orthodox world, and it accepted the influence of the various periods of Byzantine art more or less passively. For a long time all its artistic works were done by the artists of the Orthodox East. The most ancient stone churches and cathedrals in Kiev, Novgorod, and Suzdal were erected by Greek architects, while Greek painters or their conscientious Russian pupils, frequently under the masters' personal supervision, adorned these churches with frescoes, mosaics, and icons. But even in the early days some distinctly Russian traits were gradually added to the style adopted from the East. At first these innovations were introduced just as unconsciously as were the changes in the Russian church practice. Nevertheless, in these local peculiarities lay the germ of national Russian art, and so now we must study their fate.

In Russia, as everywhere else, architecture being the most material of all the branches of art and the most closely connected with everyday life, was more apt to develop independently. Of course, in any country it always depends largely upon local conditions such as climate, soil, and available building material as well as upon the customs and needs of the people. In adapting the arrangement of his rural home to local conditions the peasant did not realize that he was creating thereby a distinctive national type of building, and yet this rural home is considered by some students the prototype of the national Russian architecture. In a country so rich in forests it was natural for the original architectural style to be developed along the lines of wooden construction, while building in stone remained for a long time under foreign influence. Little is known about the constructions in stone of Kievan Russia,[1] but modern scholars presume that besides the Byzantine there was also Armenian, Georgian, and even Scandinavian influence. In fact, the South Russian cathedrals were built by foreign artisans and no national Russian influence can be traced there.

The question of Novgorod and Pskov architecture is another matter. A foreign influence existed there too which, coming from the West, brought with it the aftermath of the Romanesque style. But low and stockily built Novgorod churches, with their intersected double-sloped roofs, forming a gable on each side of the four sides of the cube, which replaced the pedimental covering of the southern churches, already bore evidence of the effect of the local climate and the influence of wooden architecture. Thus the original traits acquired by ecclesiastical architecture in Russia became apparent in this style. By passing to the Vladimir-Suzdal style of architecture we find ourselves on more solid ground, for there the Romanesque, and specifically the Italian influence, is very pronounced. The peculiar characteristics of the Vladimir-Suzdal church, as compared to that of Novgorod, are its grace, its tendency to greater height, and the ever

---

[1] Here and below the geographical terms imply also a chronological difference between various periods. Thus "Kievan Russia" means Russia of the eleventh and twelfth centuries. The "Vladimir-Suzdal style" did not reach its full development until the thirteenth and fourteenth centuries, while "Moscow architecture" refers to the architecture of the fifteenth–seventeenth centuries.—ED.

increasing ornamentation on the walls, which in Novgorod are plain. The Vladimir-Suzdal church has a Romanesque portal, and at the level of the second story a row of small arches and columns; at times it is also decorated with sculptured ornament, as, for instance, the Church of the Intercession and the Cathedrals of St. Dmitry and of St. George. Indeed, the peculiarities of the Suzdal style did not emanate from the national architecture, and even the most zealous defenders of native originality in the Russian art of building, in order not to acknowledge a Western influence, could only try to prove that they were of Asiatic origin. It is quite possible, however, that they were merely a product of new Russian adoptions from Byzantium, which by that time had established new forms of ornament and architecture. In Byzantium these new forms assimilated the Eastern and Western (Italian) influences, and also served as the intermediary link in the influence of the East on the West, while in Suzdal Russia the new peculiarities were but more or less successful copies of foreign patterns. However, whether it was the Romanesque, Indian, or any other style, whether it had come to Russia through Novgorod, Byzantium, or perhaps the southern steppes, it was not the indigenous style, the characteristics of which we want to trace in Russian architecture.

In its early stage Moscow architecture was merely an imitation of that of Suzdal. When Ivan III invited famous Italian architects to erect churches in the Kremlin, he bade them adhere strictly to the ancient Russian types of stone construction. Thus the Cathedral of the Assumption in Moscow, built in 1475–79 by Rodolfo Fioravanti (surnamed Aristotle), in its outer form varies only slightly from the Suzdal style.

But during this same period (1490) another cathedral, that of the Annunciation, was constructed in the Kremlin by some Russian artisans from Pskov. In this instance for the first time a new element, which did not originate either in the East or West but in the forms of local wooden style, penetrated into the Moscow stone architecture. Towards the middle of the sixteenth century Russian artisans frequently copied the wooden forms in stone. The most remarkable monument of this new national style is the Cathedral of St. Basil the Blessed (Vasily Blazhenny).

In order to explain how new Russian forms were introduced into the old Byzantine style, we must dwell on one of the most striking instances, the history of roof construction in the Russian churches.

In architecture the question of vaulting and roof covering was always one of the most important problems, upon the solution of which depended the style of the building. During the flourishing epoch (VI–VII centuries) of Byzantine art, the vaulting of the church roof was in the form of a hemisphere, resting directly on the "shoulders" of the church (figure I, the dome of St. Sophia in Constantinople). At the time of the second flourishing period (IX–X centuries), the introduction of a "neck" or "drum" upon which the hemispherical dome could rest made the roof appear less heavy and better proportioned (figure II, the dome of the Church of Theotocos in Constantinople). During the third brilliant period (XIII–XV centuries)—that of the local Greek-Slavonic national styles—the "drum" acquired a slenderer, still better proportion. These last two forms of Byzantine domes had been adopted in Russia. It is true that but a few roofs of the ancient churches of Kievan Russia have been preserved, and are only being hypothetically reconstructed after the sketch in figure II. But the Suzdal style of architecture adhered to the old flat type of roof (figure III, St. Dmitry's Cathedral in Vladimir). However, even in the ancient Russian manuscripts of the twelfth and fourteenth centuries there are drawings of a different form of cupola, one that is popular to the present day (figure IV, a drawing from a manuscript of the year 1100). The Byzantine dome was transformed into the Russian "bulb" by inflating the sides of the hemisphere so as to overhang the drum, while the upper part of the cupola was brought together into a point (figure V). Of course, similar forms existed in Eastern art as well, and are to be found in the Moslem and at times even in Western architecture, but there is also a parallel to it in the local wooden structures of ancient Russia, where wooden buildings with an oblong plan were roofed by a "cask," or ridged roof in sections like an ogee or a horseshoe. Sometimes there were two intersecting casks (figure VI) or the four edges of a cask-roof were joined together directly over the square space and

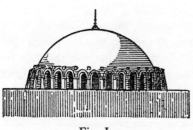

Fig. I

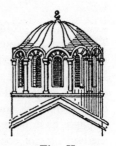

Fig. II

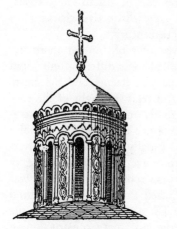

Fig. III

Fig. IV

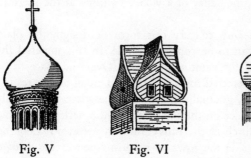

Fig. V

Fig. VI

Fig. VII

following the profile of the edge assumed the shape of a cube.
This form of roof greatly resembled the bulb-shaped dome
(figure VII) and even more so when the roof was not joined over
a square but over a polygonal "drum." In this case the roof acquired a polygonal form, although preserving the characteristics
of both the cask and the cube (figure VIII).

There have been many disputes among scholars whether this
method of roof construction on wooden churches had produced
the Russian bulb-shaped dome or whether its appearance was due
to some other influence. However, the further penetration of
wooden forms into stone structures can be traced quite easily.
It was precisely this process that gave distinctive character to
Moscow architecture of the sixteenth century.

The cask was an ornamental type of roof, but far more frequent, of course, were the plain gabled roofs differing only from
the modern ones in that their slope was steeper and the entire
roof rose higher. The steep slope and relative height of the roof
caused the moisture to fall more rapidly and easily, thus preserving the roof from decay. The flat cornice that edged it was also
adapted to climatic conditions and usually was broad and over-
lapped far over the walls in order to protect them from the heavy
drip of water. The high, steep Russian roof with its cornice was
placed over the rectangle and acquired the form of a pyramid
resting upon a broad base (figure IX, a wooden church in the
province of Olonetsk). This was the customary construction in
old Russian churches, and was called the "tent." Sometimes the
tent and cask were combined and formed a new and very beautiful roof (figure X, the belfry of a wooden church at the Hermitage of Gethsemane).

During the sixteenth century this form of design, the plain
tent and cask, began to be copied in stone. In this material the
cask was also used for vaulting purposes. Over the space to be
covered there were erected rows and rows of small arches resting
one upon the other, gradually narrowing the space until finally
it was possible to place on the top a tent or the neck of a cupola
(figure XI, the church of the Intercession in Moscow). Looking
at it from the outside the rows of superimposed arches (koko-
shniks), sometimes perfectly rounded, sometimes pointed at the

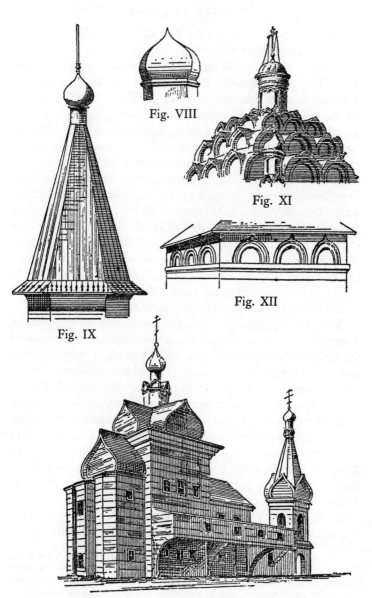

Fig. VIII

Fig. XI

Fig. IX

Fig. XII

Fig. X

top, or so inflated on the sides that they resembled a wooden cask, produced a most picturesque effect.

We have said that the end of the fifteenth century was the time when purely Russian forms of roof construction were introduced into the Moscow style. In building the Cathedral of the Annunciation the artisans from Pskov for the first time copied the cask-shaped roof with superimposed arch effect in stone, but used Italian motifs in the ornamentation of portals and windows. That was the period when successive Russian embassies (1484, 1488, 1493, 1499–1504, 1527) imported architects from Northern Italy to work on the Kremlin walls and cathedrals. Alevisio Nuovi, a Milanese, built the Archangel's Cathedral (1505–09) and the lower story of the "Terem" Palace (1508).[2] Antonio Solario, his fellow countryman, in collaboration with Marco Ruffo, built the Granovitaia Palata in the Kremlin, modeling it upon Palazzo Bevilacqua in Bologna, and the walls and lower stories of the towers of the Kremlin, which they copied from the Castello Sforzesco in Milan.

However, immediately upon the completion of the "Italian Kremlin," Russian artisans, who in the meantime had mastered the foreign technique and now wanted to show their skill, began without hesitation to adapt the national wooden forms to stone construction. From the twenties of the sixteenth century these adaptations met with increasing popularity. Over the superimposed arches was erected a high stone tent, lending the appearance of a well-proportioned tower to the church (figure XIII, the church in the village of Kolomenskoe near Moscow, 1520). Then the central tower was surrounded by small towers of the same type, and the superimposed arches and drums were given a more fanciful form (figure XIV, the church in the village of Diakovo, 1529). Thus the ground was prepared for the most original creation of Russian architecture, the Cathedral of St.

---

[2] The old Russian word "terem" had several meanings. In some cases it was used to designate the upper parts of a dwelling or more specifically the living quarters occupied by the womenfolk. In other cases, as in this one, it was used in a wider sense, being applied to the whole mansion. According to recent investigations, Alevisio Nuovi was responsible only for the Archangel's Cathedral, while the Terem Palace was built by another Alevisio who came to Russia about the same time.—Ed.

Fig. XIII

Fig. XIV

Basil the Blessed (1555), which was built by Postnik and Barma, two Russian artisans who, in the words of the contemporary chronicles, were "wise and facile in such wondrous work." It is clear that neither the West nor India gave birth to this peculiar style, but that its characteristics descended directly from the motifs of Russian wooden architecture.

Thus, towards the middle of the sixteenth century, the principal elements of an original Russian architectural style were definitely established. In relation to the traditional Byzantine style the introduction of these elements was an unforgivable innovation not to be tolerated by the church. Anything was wrong that exceeded the limits of the long-established Byzantine patterns, and in order to be faithful to them Tsar Ivan III had Aristotle Fioravanti copy those of Suzdal. With the same effects in view the government of the seventeenth century repeatedly decreed that the style of the Cathedral of the Assumption, erected under Ivan III, should be copied, but

. . . not transformed to suit the artist's own ideas. . . . In observance of the rules of the Holy Apostles and the Fathers the Lord's church should have five cupolas and not resemble a tent. . . . It should be built conforming to regulative and statutory law as prescribed by the rules and statutes of the church, and should be a one, or three, or five-domed, but never a tent-shaped church . . . neither should the cupola have the shape of a tent.

As we may observe, the national traits in ecclesiastical architecture shared the same fate as the national traits in the practices of the Russian church. During the sixteenth century both flourished and played a prominent part, but in the seventeenth century they were condemned as treasonable to Byzantine tradition.[3] The national life, which was already lacking in spiritual content, became even sadder when all that was national was condemned as being wrong.

Some opposition to the Moscow decrees was manifested in the upper Volga region. During the second part of the seventeenth century Iaroslavl became a prosperous city because of its loca-

[3] For the parallel development in the field of religion, see Part I, chs. 2 and 3.—ED.

tion at the crossroads, where the waterway of the Volga met the
busy commercial road connecting Moscow with the only seaport
at Archangel. Rich Iaroslavl merchants, wanting to immortal-
ize their names, erected spacious churches, and although they
did not dare dispense with the prescribed five-dome type, they
compensated for it by building around the central quadrangle of
the church gorgeous galleries, portals, and tent-shaped bell towers, and decorating the outside walls with ornaments in brick
and tile, and the interior with frescoes. The Iaroslavl style was
also adopted in Rostov, Borisoglebsk, and Uglich. Altogether
these patterns of northern architecture form a separate chapter
in the history of Russian art.

The instinct for national architecture, however, was not sufficiently strong to resist official pressure. Therefore the tent-
shaped roof was built only on bell towers, and the superimposed
arches, so popular with the Russian architects, gradually lost their
former structural importance and as mere ornaments found shelter
under the church's roof (figure XII, the church of the Annunciation in the village of Taininskoe, near Moscow). Thus, at the time
when the West began to exercise a particularly strong influence
over Russian architecture the latter had already lost much of its
national content. It is difficult to say what would have been the
result of Western influence had the Russian architects retained
enough originality with which to oppose it. As it was it led to
the copying of foreign designs, while the national traits were relegated to oblivion.

Since the time of Peter I a new influx of foreign influences—
German, French, Italian, and English—entered the field of Russian architecture as it did the other spheres of Russian cultural
life. The traces of these influences were more marked in architecture, because the new capital offered a wide scope for construction in modern styles. The inexhaustible means possessed
by the court at St. Petersburg,[4] the most extravagant among contemporary European courts, made it possible to invite the best
masters from abroad for the realization of great projects. The
dignitaries and favorites of the moment followed the example of

[4] St. Petersburg became the capital of Russia in the early eighteenth century during the reign of Peter the Great.—ED.

the court and commissioned the artists to build palaces in town and on their large country estates, modeling them on the architectural forms accepted at the capital.

Indeed this art, even more than that of other epochs, was beyond the comprehension or requirements of the masses, and therefore it is impossible to allude to it as national. But, after the studies of Igor Grabar and A. Benois, it is equally impossible to regard it as purely imitative and unworthy of attention. The Western styles of architecture changed constantly, and Russian patrons and architects, though somewhat belatedly, followed the newest European fashion. In Europe, during the early part of the eighteenth century, the Baroque was replaced by the Palladian, and in its second half a purer classical style was introduced, which at the beginning of the nineteenth century developed into Empire, the strictly Hellenic style. Russia too passed through all these stages and, as shall be seen, the architectural problems connected with each style were not always solved there by foreign masters but often in collaboration with Russians, who had studied art abroad and brought back to their native country not only the knowledge they had acquired, but also their own talents, which in many instances equaled those of the foreigners. Thus the art of building did not die in Russia even during the imitative period of the eighteenth century; quite the contrary, it gave to posterity new achievements, never seen before. Like all the culture of Russia in the eighteenth and the first quarter of the nineteenth centuries, both branches of stone architecture, the ecclesiastical and secular, the latter of which was almost novel in the history of Russia, were developed under the standard of cosmopolitanism. But they developed on local ground and in them, naturally, were reflected all local peculiarities.

For more than a century St. Petersburg was the chief center of architectural experiments. From the days of Peter the Great to those of Nicholas I (1825–55) the northern capital remained the "city of palaces surrounded by wastelands" that Diderot found in 1773. State authorities exercised the same unlimited control over metropolitan construction at the time when the Architectural Committee of Alexander I sanctioned or rejected plans and drawings for the façades of buildings and regulated the layout

of streets and squares according to the Emperor's command, as
they did in the days of Peter the Great, when the Chancery for
Construction (1719) decreed that the citizens were "not to fail
to use stone or at least to imitate bricks when painting" the
"model" houses which had to be built according to plans drawn
especially "for the mean, the wealthy, and the most noble" by
the Italian architect Trezzini. Moreover, it must be remembered
that Peter the Great, Catherine II, and Alexander I each had a
true mania for building. In fact, Peter was most anxious to
build St. Petersburg, and finding that "stone construction here
is much too slow" forbade "the building of stone houses throughout the Empire, under the threat of confiscation of all property
and banishment." He wished to have his capital equal the residences of foreign sovereigns. In 1779 Catherine II, writing to
Grimm, thus described the passion for construction: "At this
moment there is raging here a fury for building worse than at
any other time, and I doubt that earthquakes could ever have
demolished as many structures as we are erecting. . . . It is
clearly a disease, somewhat like tippling." Alexander I too shared
this passion, and even took the plans and sketches with him on
his wanderings through Europe. "He intended making St. Petersburg more beautiful than all the capitals he visited in Europe,"
wrote Vigel.

Indeed, in St. Petersburg with its "wastelands" the foreign and
Russian architects found far greater opportunity than at any
other capital for developing many most extravagant projects.
Consequently, in one hundred years it was transformed from
a "city of wastelands" into one of monumental edifices adapted
for state and social requirements but not for private dwelling. It
is true that Custine, in his well-known work *La Russie en 1839*
stated that all these buildings, with their colonnades and horizontal lines transplanted from cloudless Italy and Hellas to the
marshy land of misty and rainy St. Petersburg, disturbed the
harmony of the landscape. Nevertheless this architecture char-
acterized most vividly the epoch of enlightened absolutism,
which had broken the bonds of tradition and which, not having
as yet found its own national ground, was living surrounded by
gallantry and luxury in the atmosphere of foreign culture.

The transition from the epoch of national architecture prior to Peter I to the imitative period of his reign is marked by the peculiar adaptation in Moscow of the late Renaissance or Baroque style, so popular in Europe during the seventeenth century. The characteristics of this style manifest a decline from the artistic simplicity of the Renaissance and the predominance of the decorative over the structural motifs. In it the straight line is replaced by a curve, the pediments are broken in the center and take the form of a curved line, or are replaced by "shields" independent of the roof, while the walls, capitals, and window frames are encumbered more and more with elaborate cast ornaments. The Baroque style, in spite of its derogatory name meaning "curved, odd, irregular," had its merits and provided unlimited possibilities for the new and original creations. It was brought to Muscovite Russia during the last part of the seventeenth century from Poland by way of the Ukraine. Baroque had a period of development in the Ukraine and left many remarkable monuments which testify that the local architecture, which at first had acquired some traits of this style, in turn exerted an influence upon it. The best periods in the Ukrainian Baroque are associated with the names of Peter Mogila, in the middle, and Hetman Mazepa at the end of the seventeenth century. It is interesting to notice that during the latter part of the century the Ukraine first sent to Moscow her architects, expert in this style.

Peter the Great, having repudiated the old Moscow style, could not escape entirely the influence of the new one that had equally been adopted from the West. Yet he did not build in the Baroque style already introduced into Russia from the Ukraine, but in the one brought directly from its source or, to be precise, from several sources. It is therefore impossible to call the style of Peter's time a special Russian variation of Baroque. Under Peter, North German and Dutch traits were prevalent in Russian architecture not only because the Emperor was more familiar with them, but also because his chief architect Domenico Trezzini, of Swiss-Italian origin, had acquired during his many years of service at the court of the King of Denmark a preference for Northern Baroque. Trezzini was responsible for the first monumental buildings—the Cathedral and Fortress of SS. Peter and

Paul, the house of the Twelve Colleges (subsequently the St. Petersburg University), and a part of the Alexander Nevsky Abbey—and the famous steeples of St. Petersburg. Peter had succeeded also in retaining for Russia the services of Schlueter, the famous architect of the Royal Palace at Berlin, but Schlueter died the year following his arrival (1714). Leblond, a French architect, who also came at Peter's invitation, lived only three years in St. Petersburg, and died in 1719. After failing in his fantastic scheme to transform the wastelands of St. Petersburg into the semblance of a French garden with Venetian canals instead of thoroughfares, Leblond drew plans for the Summer Garden and the gardens of Peterhof and Strelna, but all his works are preserved only in drawings. The German architect Schedel was more fortunate, because some of his works still exist as, for instance, the two palaces he built for Menshikov, one on Basil Island in St. Petersburg (subsequently the military school) and the other in Oranienbaum.

The general impression which the new capital created remained unchanged until Empress Elizabeth acceded to the throne (1741). In 1739 Algarotti, an Italian, said: "There prevails a mixed type of architecture in this capital, suggesting those of Italy, France, and Holland, with the Dutch predominating." Elizabeth, with her love of luxury and grandeur, supplied the incentive to the further architectural development of St. Petersburg. It was during her reign that Baroque acquired some new traits, known as "Rococo" (style of the Regency and Louis XV), which in Russia is associated with the name of the famous Rastrelli, who took his ideas both from France, where he had studied, and from Southern Germany, where the Rococo style was particularly overladen with decorative elements. Rastrelli's architectural works are exceedingly numerous; he worked for the Empress and those immediately surrounding her, and there were but a few wealthy landowners who could not boast of having copied Rastrelli's style in their country estates. The most famous among his works are the palaces in Peterhof and Tsarskoe Selo, which he reconstructed, the first in 1747 and the second in 1749, the Winter Palace which he designed and built in 1754–62, the Cathedral at the Smolny Convent, part of the grandiose plan that was never carried out, and the graceful Cathedral of St. Andrew at Kiev, beautifully situated on the slope of a mountain above the Podol. Then there are the palaces built by him for the dignitaries, such as the Anichkov Palace, originally Razumovsky's, Count M. I. Vorontsov's (subsequently the Corps des Pages), and Count S. G. Stroganov's—the last two remarkable for their noble proportions and their façades artistically divided by pilasters and projecting bays.

Until the reign of Catherine II (1762-96) the part played by Russian architects, as compared to that of the foreign masters, was most insignificant. The first Russian to gain renown in this field was Michael Zemtsov, who as a boy was brought from Moscow to the newly founded St. Petersburg, where he was taught Italian in order to serve as interpreter to the foreign artists. Having studied architecture under Trezzini, Zemtsov worked as assistant architect with Leblond's successor Michetti, and only after the latter had left Russia (1728) was the young Russian promoted to the rank of chief architect. Peter the Great had also commissioned about a dozen young men to study art abroad, but of them all only Eropkin subsequently attained fame. Zemtsov left two works to posterity, the church of St. Simeon and St. Anna on Mokhovaia Street—an imitation of Trezzini's Cathedral of SS. Peter and Paul—and the graceful memorial building erected to house the yawl of Peter the Great.[5] He died in 1743 and Rastrelli replaced him in the work of palace construction.

The Academy of Arts, founded in 1758 by Empress Elizabeth, became the veritable nursery of Russian artists. It was permanently organized under Catherine II, when Betskoy in 1774 drew up its statutes, copying almost exactly those of the Paris Academy. The professors of architecture, sculpture, and painting were Frenchmen, and therefore their methods of instruction were, naturally, purely French. The graduates of the Academy were sent to finish their studies abroad—mostly in Paris. In spite of this, upon their return the young Russian artists played only a secondary part, for Catherine still continued to invite the out-

[5] The famous small boat the acquaintance with which stimulated young Peter's interest in shipbuilding and navigation. It was preserved as a historical relic.—ED.

standing foreign masters to Russia. These invitations resulted in all the styles that were succeeding each other in Europe, especially in France, being reproduced in Russia more rapidly during the latter half of the eighteenth century than in former days.

The transition from the ornate Rococo to the classical style of Palladio shows the personal taste of Catherine II, who preferred simplicity and comfort to the ostentatious luxury that Elizabeth had favored. During the early period of her reign Empress Catherine II profited by the presence in St. Petersburg of Vallin de la Mothe, a professor at the Paris Academy, to have some buildings erected in her favorite style. Vallin de la Mothe was a follower of the famous Gabriel, architect of the École Militaire and the buildings on the Place de la Concorde; he remained in St. Petersburg until 1775 and with the assistance of Kokorinov, a Russian architect, built the Academy of Arts and the "Old Hermitage" (the part adjacent to the Winter Palace). But there is still another work of his which has been preserved, the rounded corner of the Gostiny Dvor (Merchants' Row), facing Nevsky Prospekt and Sadovaia Street.

In 1752 Antonio Rinaldi was brought from Rome by Hetman Razumovsky and was appointed by Empress Elizabeth as court architect to the heir apparent, Grand Duke Peter. He was entrusted with building the miniature palaces at Oranienbaum, one of which, the "Chinese," with particularly gorgeous decorations, is still well preserved. This was followed with other far more important tasks, for during the year 1766 Rinaldi completed the Gatchina Palace and in 1768 the Marble Palace, both of which were Empress Catherine's gifts to Gregory Orlov.

In the interim, between the period when Russia was infatuated with everything that was foreign and the one that followed, three Russians, pupils of foreign celebrities, were commissioned by Catherine II to execute some work. They were Veldten, a Russianized German, the son of Peter's chief kitchen steward, and Bazhenov and Starov, two pupils of de la Mothe and the first graduates of the Academy to be sent to Paris with a scholarship. Veldten, who had finished his studies in Germany and obtained his architect's diploma in 1760, was commissioned to face the left bank of the Neva "from the Summer House to the

Galerny Palace," with granite. It took him over twenty years to accomplish this task, but he did it with outstanding talent and contributed to St. Petersburg one of its greatest adornments. The famous decorative fence of the Summer Garden, in which classic simplicity is combined with impressive dignity, lent a finishing touch to this work. Among Veldten's other works are the "Second Hermitage," built in line with de la Mothe's, though more simple, and seven of the St. Petersburg churches having colonnades and rotundas. In 1765 Bazhenov, who had studied under de Wailly and was member of three Italian academies, returned to St. Petersburg and immediately was entrusted with the important task of erecting the Kamenny Ostrov Palace. This building is constructed in subdued classical style without any Parisian innovations, on the same lines as the "Old Arsenal," which in 1769 he had built by Orlov's order. But Bazhenov met with cruel disappointment when his great scheme of covering huge areas with classical edifices in the style of the new French school (Peyre, Ledoux, Gondouin), failed to be realized. He drew up two vast plans which were never used, one for the Smolny Institute in St. Petersburg and the other for the huge Kremlin Palace in Moscow, which was to gird the entire hill and surround all the buildings of the Kremlin. Due to this failure the historic face of the fifteenth-seventeenth century Kremlin has been preserved. In St. Petersburg Bazhenov only collaborated with Brenna in the erection of Michael Castle (subsequently the Engineers' College) in which Emperor Paul I was slain. Although Starov stayed in Paris a shorter period than Bazhenov, his time there was spent with more profit, and upon his return to Russia in 1768 he was destined to achieve more lasting fame. He built the Cathedral of the Holy Trinity at the Alexander Nevsky Abbey in the form of a basilica, but it is his masterpiece, the Taurida Palace, that has preserved his name for posterity. It was built in 1788 by the Empress' command for Potemkin,[6] and in its time served as a model for many a nobleman's manor, because everyone was anxious to copy the palace of the great Prince of Taurida, with its classic portal, its colonnade on the central

[6] One of the outstanding statesmen of the period and for a while a favorite of Catherine II.—ED.

façade, its domed roof, its two wings, a theatre, and a church. The only change that was usually introduced in the country manors was a second colonnade at the rear facing the garden, with stairs that had to lead to water, whether it was a river or an artificial lake.

Starov was in advance of his time working as he did in the pure Hellenic style, which Catherine was anxious to introduce but which was only definitely established under Alexander I. In 1779 Catherine II wrote to Grimm "the French build bad houses, because they know too much." The jest meant that the Empress was tired of the old style and wanted to pass from imitation of classics to the original source. She anxiously awaited the arrival of two Italians whom she had commissioned Grimm to send. One of these two, Giacomo Quarenghi, a Roman, came to Russia in 1780 and during the reign of Catherine played the same part that Rastrelli had played in the days of Rococo, under Empress Elizabeth.

But before she fell under the sway of Quarenghi, Catherine had another period of artistic enthusiasm. In 1779 Charles Cameron, a Scotsman, arrived in St. Petersburg and absolutely fascinated the Empress with his knowledge of the classical Roman monuments. She prized him as the editor of Palladio's book on Roman baths, and always associated him with Clerisseau, the famous expert on Pompeian interior decoration, in whose books Cameron had found his inspiration. "This sparkling mind," Catherine wrote to Grimm in 1780, "is a great admirer of Clerisseau, whose sketches help Cameron in decorating my new apartments." Having put Cameron to the test by commissioning him to build the "classical pavilion" in the park, the Empress entrusted him (1780–85) with the reconstruction of her private apartments in the cold, formal palace built at Tsarskoe Selo by Empress Elizabeth, and then (1782–85) with the erection of a palace in Pavlovsk for Grand Duke Paul and Grand Duchess Marie, who under the name of Count and Countess du Nord were at that time traveling abroad. Both tasks were most brilliantly executed by Cameron. The hanging garden at Tsarskoe Selo, whose "agate rooms" situated above the bath house were sumptuously decorated, the long glass gallery, a colonnade built on the same level over a high stereobate for the Sovereign's daily walks, and the tremendous slope which the aged Empress could ascend and descend in a bath chair—everything was especially designed for her personal comfort. The palace at Pavlovsk, in the building of which Cameron was assisted by Brenna, had semicircular galleries resembling those of the Palladian villas in Northern Italy, and became a very popular model for houses in Moscow and for country homes of wealthy landowners. In contrast to the classical exterior, Cameron decorated the interior in the refined Baroque style of the eighteenth century.

Quarenghi, the Italian, having studied the original classical monuments, came nearer to true classicism and soon dimmed Cameron's fame. In this pure classical style he built in 1781-89 the English Palace in Peterhof, and in 1783-87 the Academy of Science in St. Petersburg. The façade of the third and last part of the Hermitage, that of the theatre, facing the Palace Quay, built by him in 1782-85, is less pure though more picturesque. The State Bank building (1783-88) is also imposing, but Quarenghi attained his greatest and most artistic effect in the harmony of pure lines and noble proportions of the Alexander Palace at Tsarskoe Selo (1792-96).

Quarenghi continued to work under Paul and Alexander I, adapting his art to the tastes of each sovereign while preserving always his own individuality. For Paul I he built the Horse Guards' Riding Hall and the church of the Order of Malta; for Alexander I the Smolny and Catherine Institutes. The classical colonnades at the barracks, banks, and schools were always beautiful but not characteristic of the special purpose to which the buildings were assigned. Classicism prevailed everywhere, thus emphasizing that the work was done by official commission.

During the reign of Alexander I the Louis XVI style gave place to that of the Empire, which was the last step in the development of classical form. The enthusiasm for Rome was replaced with an ardent admiration for Hellas. While the Pantheon still preserved its fascination, the ruins of the Doric temple in Paestum became the architects' ideal. The tendency towards extreme simplicity of line was combined with the passion for colossal dimensions. The names of Piranesi and Ledoux were characteristic of this style and of the period of its origin in France, from which, after a delay of thirty years, it reached Russia in the days of Alexander I. In Western Europe the very grandeur of the best projects, even under Napoleon, impeded their realization. But Russia, with its imperial commissions, particularly in St. Petersburg, proved to be the most suitable ground for the development of the new trend.

The Kazan Cathedral, the first monumental edifice erected under Alexander I (1801–11), did not as yet mark the coming of the new era. It was built by Voronikhin, a Russian architect, who as a serf of Count Stroganov was sent by him to study architecture in Paris. While it is quite evident that Voronikhin in building the Kazan Cathedral copied Bernini's colonnade of St. Peter's in Rome and that he availed himself of the sketches of Peyre senior, the architect of the Odeon, one must nevertheless admire his work. Far more original and interesting is the Doric colonnade of the Institute of Mining, which Voronikhin built in 1806–11.

Thomas de Thomon, a French émigré who was responsible for the Grand Theatre (1802–05) and the St. Petersburg Stock Exchange (the lines and rostral columns of the latter were adopted from the project of Pierre Bernard for which he received a prize in 1792), was a true representative of the new Russian style. The Stock Exchange, which stands on the point of an island amid the open waters of the Neva, completes the panorama of St. Petersburg and produces a powerful and monumental effect. Thomon had a rival in Zakharov, a Russian follower of Ledoux and Chalgrin, who during the years 1806–15 built the Admiralty in St. Petersburg. We must also mention Stasov's barracks of the Pavlovsk regiment (1817–18), the imperial stables (1817–23), the Cathedrals of the Transfiguration (1826–28) and of the Holy Trinity (1827–35), and the arch at the Moscow Gate (1833–38).

But Carlo Rossi was the man who crowned the Alexander style and the entire St. Petersburg period in architecture. Rossi was the illegitimate son of an Italian dancer of the days of Empress Catherine II; he studied in Florence, but upon the death of the three foreign architects mentioned above (1811-14) he returned to Russia and gained fame. He profited by the dictatorship of the Committee for Building, which controlled all construction in St. Petersburg, to carry out Ledoux's great projects, and gave its final contemporary appearance to the monumental St. Petersburg. Rossi did not limit his work to buildings, but also planned streets and squares. The Michael Palace with its great square (1819-23), the semicircle of buildings with the famous arch in the center, facing the Winter Palace (1819-29), the square and surrounding streets at the Alexandrine Theatre, and the two connected buildings—the Senate and Synod—are the four most important examples of his ability to plan. There are some who disagree about the merits of that stately building, the Michael Palace, but no one can deny that the buildings of the General Staff, the Ministries of Foreign Affairs and of Finance with the Gate of Victory, dividing the semicircle, form a most beautiful ensemble.

The Cathedral of St. Isaac, which also belongs to the same grand style, was built by Montferrand, a French "draftsman" who had studied at the French school of Perier and Fontaine. It took forty years to build (1817-57) and when completed the Cathedral looked far more massive than on the plan. In the wealth of mosaics and marble and the colossal size of its pillars the St. Petersburg copy had attempted to outshine its prototypes, St. Paul's Cathedral in London and the Paris Pantheon, but *materia superavit opus:* cumbersome material overpowered the creative genius. Another work of Montferrand, the Alexander Column, the highest that was ever made in monolith, was intended by Emperor Nicholas I to surpass the Vendôme Column in Paris, but likewise failed to attain the purpose. With Rossi and the gigantic St. Isaac Cathedral the magnificent architectural pageant that had been unfolded in St. Petersburg came to an end. Under Nicholas I absolutism ceased to be enlightened and grew cold to refinements in art, while the requirements of everyday life, hitherto ignored by the monumental style, became too urgent to be neglected. St. Petersburg was no longer a "wasteland."

Architecture ceased to pursue the pompous, spacious, grand style in building; there was an increased demand for comfortably planned apartments, good lighting conditions, etc., which were incompatible with the adopted type of classical temple, with its colonnade, portico, and great wall space. To comply with the practical requirements of life, the façades were now divided into stories, more and higher windows were pierced leaving less wall space, while the number of pediments and cornices increased; in a word, there was a general degeneration which, as usual, was accompanied by the development of detail. Finally, throughout Europe there arose a national movement, which made the new architecture seek for motifs in national art. (Fomin)

In the Russia of the days of Emperor Nicholas I this mood was expressed by a new imperial "command." There were published official albums of "façades for buildings in the cities of the Russian Empire approved and sanctioned by His Majesty." The new "social command" was not to outdo the foreigners by imitating them but, with His Majesty's sanction, to create a new national Russian style.

During the thirties of the nineteenth century the government officially exacted this style of the artists. The command was executed by Thon, who added to Russian architecture a great many colorless and uninspired imitations of the ancient Moscow style. The five-domed quasi-Byzantine church, which during the seventeenth century had superseded the national Russian type, now became the prototype of a national form.

True, the matter did not end with Thon's official patterns. In studying the ancient architectural works the artists became familiar with the elements of the genuine national style, and the architectural art in the middle of the nineteenth century strove to adapt it to modern requirements. The chronicle of these efforts is written in stone on the streets of Moscow. There one sees simple copies of ancient Russian forms alongside entirely foreign ones (the Historical Museum), a reflection of the learned theory on the Russian style originating from the East (the Polytechnical Museum), a rather unsuccessful attempt at adapting the ancient Russian forms to the requirements of a modern public (the Town Hall), and quite close by a far more successful and free solution of the problems of combining the national style with the contemporary demands for comfort and good taste (the Merchants' Row).

Thus for a short time in returning to the traditions of the sixteenth century Russian architecture found its way to independent development. But this effort had to yield its place rapidly to greater tasks. Viollet-le-Duc was the first to predict the advance of steel architecture, but actually it developed into steel and concrete. This time both the style and building material were international, but we shall study this subject later on. Thus the experiment of re-creating the national style came to an end, and in Russian art its elements retained exclusively a decorative value.

II

PAINTING: TO THE MIDDLE OF THE
NINETEENTH CENTURY

THE other branches of art in Russia were in a different position for they did not have such palpable, objective, and original forms at their disposal as had architecture. Only the ornament, being in a somewhat similar state, shared its fate. Besides the purely architectural ornaments of wooden and more modern brick construction, there were many to be found in ancient Russian manuscripts and to be adopted by the national industry. As early as the fourteenth century there appeared in Russia a peculiar ornament of intricate design with forms of animals, which can also be found both in the Western "monster" and the Eastern styles. During the fifteenth century this was replaced by a geometrical one, at times very complicated, which by repeating the motif could, like the arabesque, be used to cover large surfaces. In the sixteenth century still another type of ornament was introduced, a solid and somewhat heavy design executed in gilt and many colors, in which foliage appeared along with the geometrical forms, while towards the end of the sixteenth and the beginning of the seventeenth centuries this foliage was outlined and shaded in the manner of foreign prints.

In no other branch of Russian art except architecture can a similar perfection and vitality of ancient forms be found. We know the circumstances which even in Byzantium arrested the progress of Christian sculpture. In pagan Russia the fear that statues might be taken for idols was, of course, more natural than in Byzantium, which was accustomed to classical forms of art. Carved works, not only as objects of worship in church, but even as simple adornments in private houses caused great disturbance and strong disapproval. The Muscovites were very indignant when Pseudo-Dmitry [1] erected a statue of Hades in front of his palace. "It is not fitting for an Orthodox Christian to place fantastic beasts, dragons, or any valiant infidel knight above the gates of the house," reads the illuminated church calendar of the seventeenth century. "Orthodox Christians should place above the house gates either holy icons or crosses." With such an attitude towards sculpture this branch of figurative art was almost non-existent in ancient Russia except in the Ukraine, where sculpture had been introduced from Poland, and in the far north, where up to recent times the natives worshiped as idols their gods carved in wood.

It was not until the first quarter of the twentieth century that it became possible to study the most ancient period (XII–XV centuries) of Russian religious art—the frescoes, icons, and mosaics; only since 1904 has scientific study begun to replace the hypothetical knowledge of the former icon collectors. The principle of this study was to restore the ancient monuments to their original state by removing the layers of paint, drawings, and stucco that had been superimposed. The work of restoration progressed particularly successfully when expert scholars were allowed free access to church relics. After 1918 the workers of the State Central Restoration Work Rooms—in most cases the same men who had inaugurated these studies before the revolution—extended their research to a number of churches and icons, where they could expect to find the most ancient examples of Byzantine and Russian art. Indeed, it proved possible to restore to their original state, to date and compare with each other many invaluable works of art which had been inaccessible to the scholars of the earlier days. Therefore the entire history of that period must now be rewritten.

The most important achievement of this modern research is the establishment of the fact that the nationalization of the Eastern type of religious painting had taken place much earlier than was formerly believed. Among the invaluable, purely Byzantine fres-

---

[1] The mysterious pretender of the early seventeenth century who, claiming that he was a son of Ivan the Terrible, succeeded in establishing himself for a short time as Tsar in Moscow.—ED.

coes of the eleventh and twelfth centuries, painted by Greek masters in Kiev and Vladimir, and among icons brought to Russia during that period, A. I. Anisimov has discovered some new traits, which in the course of the thirteenth century were particularly clearly defined. While still adhering to the Byzantine type, the Russian pupils of the Greek masters nevertheless permitted some changes both in modeling and in the use of colors. The immediate result was a certain simplification. In Anisimov's opinion, subsequently disputed, the faces on the two icons of the Virgin of Tolgsk, both works of a Russian icon painter, "not only lack the inexhaustibly deep psychology of the Vladimir icon,[2] but even the refinement and outer nobility which distinguish the two icons of the Virgin in the New York collections. Instead they possess a sincere and spontaneous quality from which there emanates a feeling of intimacy that endows the Russian icons with a rare character of inner warmth." Simplification of the face led to simplification of the figure. The folds of the garments, which in the Byzantine images fell in undulating lines following the curves of the body, were replaced with straight lines producing the effect of a flat drawing. With the disappearance of the relief, what remained of the perspective also disappeared. It must be pointed out that, according to Anisimov, these peculiarities are first seen in the Novgorod school of icon painting, which "decidedly Russianized the faces and abandoned the Byzantine canonical prototype earlier and more definitely than did the Rostov and Suzdal schools." The Novgorod school also "showed preference for vivid and pure colors" against the dark shades and semi-tones of the Byzantine images, while the Suzdal school "even in tonality adhered more faithfully to the very ancient traditions."

Anisimov's observations are new and clever, but his deductions are, at times, hastily made. At least Schweinfurth, the most recent German student of the problem, in his conscientious summary of Russian discoveries expressed the opinion that of the eight icons of the twelfth and thirteenth centuries analyzed by Anisimov, only

[2] This remarkable Byzantine icon of the twelfth century, which in 1395 was taken from Vladimir to the Cathedral of the Assumption in Moscow, has only recently been valued at its real worth. Unquestionably it does differ from the other contemporary works of Byzantine art in the intensity of sorrow expressed in the Virgin's face.

the one representing St. John, St. George, and St. Blaise was unquestionably of Russian workmanship. In accordance with his views on the ancient period of the Byzantine Italian relations, Schweinfurth believes that the first Tolgsk Virgin was a Tuscan work of the Pisan school in the *Maniera Greca,* as were the two icons now in the New York collections. It must be added, however, that Anisimov showed more caution in his English articles [3] in which he admitted that

. . . the twelfth-century icons are so characteristically Byzantine that it is an open question whether they actually were painted in Russia and by Russians. In those of the thirteenth century it is comparatively easy to distinguish national traits of a formal nature: a somewhat stronger dynamics, a tendency towards a straight line in connection with the intensification of flatness in representation, and finally, an increasing inclination towards the use of pure and vivid color. Yet until the beginning of the fourteenth century all these characteristics found no definite expression. Their establishment marks the coming of a new period in the history of style. We think that the national character of icons was definitely formed in the middle of the fourteenth century.

This new era in icon painting followed upon the interval which coincided with the establishment of the Latin Empire in Constantinople (1204–61) by the Crusaders of the Fourth Crusade, and the Tatar invasion of Kievan Russia (1223–40). During that interval ecclesiastical architecture and the art of icon painting temporarily declined, only to revive later with renewed brilliance. Modern Russian scholars regard the fourteenth and fifteenth centuries as the period of highest development in the national religious art of Russia. This is rather an exaggerated point of view which cannot be accepted without reservations. In the first place, the flourishing period in Russian art found its direct source in the brilliant era in Byzantine art of the same centuries, called by the French scholars the third Renaissance of the Paleologi epoch. The famous mosaics at Kahrié Djami in Constantinople and the frescoes of the Mistra churches in Morea are wonderful examples of this revival. But here we come to the disputed point as to the extent of the revived art's independence in Constantinople, the source from which the

[3] See *Masterpieces of Russian Painting,* edited by Michael Farbman.

Russians had adopted it. Rovinsky was first in drawing attention to the similarity between the Russian icons of this period and the works of Cimabue, Duccio, and Giotto, the Italian masters of the end of the thirteenth and the beginning of the fourteenth centuries. The crusade that was led against Constantinople, instead of Palestine, was followed by the Venetian dominion expanding over the Ionian Isles and Crete, which remained under its power from 1204 to 1669. The prosperity of Kaffa, the Genoese colony in the Crimea, which replaced the Byzantine Chersonese, is also connected with this same epoch (1266–1475). During the fourteenth and the fifteenth centuries the influence of Venice was extended as far as the Dalmatian shores, Serbia, and Moldavia-Wallachia. Nor must we forget the flourishing period of religious art in Tirnovo, "the Second Rome" of the Bulgarian dynasty of the Asens, from which, towards the end of the fifteenth century, together with literature, ecclesiastics, and the idea of Russia's Slavonic mission, the new methods of icon painting could have penetrated to Moscow. Such were the channels through which the new revival in art might slowly have reached Russia. According to Muratov, as early as the end of the fourteenth century the famous master, Theophanes the Greek, had reproduced in Russia the methods of the Macedonian artists of the twelfth and the thirteenth centuries. It was Kondakov in particular who developed the idea of the influence of the Italian-Cretan school upon Russian icon painting, basing his theory on the fact that various types of the Virgin, such as the "Sorrowful," the "Adoring," and the "Nursing," which undoubtedly were of Italian origin, appeared in Russia during the fourteenth century.

The French scholars and Muratov raised serious objections to this point of view. They argued that the "adoration" type of the Virgin was not foreign to the Byzantine Renaissance of the Paleologi period, and that it was adopted by the Italians from Byzantium. Likewise, all the motifs and characteristics of the style which Kondakov had pointed out were to be found either in Byzantine art itself or in the classical Hellenic art from which the Paleologi Renaissance had so freely borrowed. Therefore, in the opinion of these scholars, even in the fourteenth and the fifteenth centuries Byzantium had been the only source of Russian iconography.

It seems that the solution of the problem is offered by a recent theory which represents a compromise between the two extreme points of view. In the works of Ainalov and Schweinfurth the time and character of Italian influence have been definitely established, and thereby some claims of the Byzantinists have been reconciled with facts. Indeed, since very early days, aside from Constantinople there existed another center where the East came in contact with the West. This center was Venice, where as early as the first half of the thirteenth century there was a marked Romanesque influence, which during the second half of the century was replaced by that of the early Gothic. This was that *Maniera Greca*, which had been so popular throughout Italy but was abandoned with the appearance of the fourteenth-century Italian Renaissance. Venice alone retained the taste for Byzantine icons and continued to work "in the old manner" both for its local patrons and for export to Orthodox countries. It was from this source that in the sixteenth century some of the traits of medieval Western art penetrated into Russia. During the fifteenth and sixteenth centuries the Venetian colony of Crete also began producing Byzantine icons, showing more decided traces of the Renaissance influence. This particular Italian-Cretan school, as Kondakov has pointed out, exerted a more important influence upon Russian icon painting of the Moscow period (XV–XVII centuries).

The revival of icon painting during that time is reflected in a marked increase of available historical evidence. In Russia the name of Theophanes the Greek is associated with a series of new frescoes in the cathedrals and churches of Moscow which he, with the assistance of his Russian colleagues, had painted in the years 1395–1405. True, these frescoes have perished, but on the walls of some of the Novgorod churches Theophanes' work is still preserved. It is most characteristic of the new style of the late Byzantine Renaissance with its "illusionism" (an approach towards realism), its angular movements, sharp graphics, and non-Byzantine type of faces. Indeed, we have already reached here the limits of simplification and emancipation beyond which lies the possibility for the creation of a national style.

In fact, the comparative isolation of Russia during the period between the thirteenth and fourteenth centuries contributed to the development of a national Russian style on the basis of the previously adopted Byzantine tradition. The Greco-Russian frescoes of the thirteenth and fifteenth centuries shared the fate of the gorgeous Byzantine mosaics of the eleventh century and gradually disappeared. They were replaced in the wooden churches of Northern Russia by a rapidly increasing number of icons painted on wooden panels. When there was no longer any space for the holy images in the dome, drums, wings, or on the pillars and walls of the churches, they were placed according to traditional order and "rank" upon a high iconostasis, a structure separating the body of the church from the sanctuary, which was introduced by North Russian wooden architecture and later built also in the stone churches. On either side of the "Deësis" (an icon of Christ, the Holy Virgin, and St. John the Baptist), which was placed above the "Holy Gate," were the images of Archangels and Apostles; above this "Apostolic row" were icons commemorating church holidays; in the third row, icons representing the Prophets; in the fourth row, the images of the Patriarchs; and above the entire iconostasis, the God Sabaoth. On each side of the Holy Gate were placed the local icons that were held in the highest esteem. Because of conditions in Russia, about which we already know,[4] the icon became an object of special veneration in the same superstitious sense that provoked iconoclasm in Byzantium. Everyone was anxious to possess an icon, and particularly of those saints who cured diseases, protected cattle and horses, etc. The demand for icons was so great that it resulted in a mechanical reproduction of the established types, and led to further simplification of drawing and coloring, and a still greater conventionalization of style. The pictorial style of Byzantine icon painting yielded more and more to the graphic manner, with its straight lines and sharp contours in drawing, and acquired a flat character.

Of course such sacred figures as Christ, the Virgin, and the Apostles retained their traditional outlines. Yet the artist was free to choose his colors, and these began to change before the faces on the icons were nationalized. Consequently the local schools of icon painting can be best identified through the combination of

4 See Part I, ch. 2.—ED.

colors. In painting the images of secondary saints and figures and in the composition and treatment of complex icons the artists were allowed even greater freedom. It was exactly in this field that the inner development of icon painting was achieved, although in Russia not as rapidly as in the Orthodox South.

Up to the present it is not quite clear what part was played in this development by Novgorod and Suzdal (Vladimir-Moscow), the two great political and cultural centers in the Russia of the period following upon the Tatar invasion (XIV–XV centuries). It was natural that at the beginning of this period Novgorod should become the principal center of both religious art and icon production. It was there that the largest number of churches was built, and Greek masters were continually being invited to paint them in fresco. It was there too that for the first time the works of the Greeks were supplemented or replaced by those done by masters of Russian origin, but with Greek training. Novgorod treated the Byzantine patterns with the greatest independence, and as early as the thirteenth century its art showed unmistakable signs of nationalization. This is why up to recent times everything original in the religious art of that period was ascribed to the "Novgorod School." Only during the last years have the peculiar characteristics of Suzdal icon painting begun to emerge from obscurity. It should have been realized sooner that this ancient seat of Russian culture, though remaining true to the original Byzantine tradition, could not have existed for several centuries without developing special traits of its own. We have, in fact, visible proof of that in such historical monuments as the Cathedrals of the Assumption and of St. Dmitry in Vladimir, and the church of the Intercession on the Nerl. Igor Grabar, the historian of Russian art, in comparing the Suzdal monuments to the "solid, stockily built monuments of Novgorod the Great," describes them as "simple, strong, devoid of excessive ornamentation, and astounding in their perfect proportions, refinement, and grace." In speaking of the Suzdal icons as opposed to "the monumental, rectilinear, and angular" ones of Novgorod, Grabar says that though "not of very superior craftsmanship they nevertheless possess a feeling of greater intimacy, more rounded forms, and more rhythmic character." While golden-yellow ochre predominates in Novgorod, the Suzdal icon excels in "a gamut of silvery-blue" colors, far colder but more refined that the Novgorodian "glowing tone."

The end of the fourteenth and the beginning of the fifteenth centuries was the first flourishing period of the Suzdal school and was marked by the activity of the famous artist Andrew Rublev, a monk of the Spaso-Andronikov Monastery (b. *circa* 1360–70, d. *circa* 1420–30). Igor Grabar has succeeded very recently in collecting reliable material for the study of the works of this outstanding icon painter. The most characteristic and finished of them is the icon of the Holy Trinity which he painted for the Sergievo-Troitsky Abbey, and which is famed for its harmony of color and composition. It must be pointed out that at an early stage both Rublev and his friend Daniel Cherny collaborated with Theophanes the Greek, who in 1405 had come from Novgorod at the invitation of the Muscovites to paint in fresco the Cathedral of the Annunciation at the Kremlin. Grabar also ascribes to Rublev that portion of frescoes in the Cathedral of the Assumption at Vladimir (1408), which in contrast to the antiquated pictorial brush work of his older friend Daniel Cherny is done in a conventionalized, graphic manner.

Indeed, Rublev's icon of the Holy Trinity was the first great achievement of the national art, as independent of outside influences as the works of Giotto and Duccio di Buoninsegna were of the Romanesque and neo-Hellenic schools of their day. But we must draw attention to the difference existing between the Russian and Italian achievements. While Andrew Rublev still adhered to the tradition of icon painting, Giotto and Duccio broke away from ancient methods.

The frescoes at the Cyril Therapontus Monastery in the region of Novgorod, painted by Dionysius in 1500–01, and those in the Cathedral of the Annunciation at Moscow, prove that after the time of Daniel Cherny and Andrew Rublev the development, if any, in the art of icon painting was only a further conventionalization of design.

The Annunciation frescoes, however, were destined to bring this tradition to an abrupt end, and to introduce a new note into the history of Russian icon painting. While restoring the frescoes on the porch of this Cathedral in 1882, Fartusov, the architect in charge of the work, discovered in them such striking "Italiana" that the committee for the restoration, headed by the historian Zabelin, accused Fartusov of fraud and positively forbade him to continue the work. The restoration was then entrusted to Safonov, a professional icon painter, who destroyed for all time the ancient frescoes, and nothing remains but the photographs taken of them by Fartusov. It was these photographs that enabled Kondakov to describe the frescoes as "quasi-Italian," and Grishchenko to compare the characteristic faces and gestures represented on them with the works of the Italian Quatrocento. The landscape, the facial expression, the headdress, and the manner of wearing the garments, were absolutely contrary to the tradition of Dionysius.

This breach of tradition was not confined to a single case alone. After the great fire at Moscow, in 1547, it was necessary to paint new icons for the Cathedral of the Annunciation and to redecorate the palace with frescoes. Artists were brought from Pskov to do the work, and in a short time new icons, some painted in Moscow and others at Pskov, replaced the old ones. But the Muscovites were disturbed by these images and Viskovaty, Ivan IV's state secretary and one of the best-educated men of the day, indignantly expressed to the Tsar his doubts as to the merits of the new trend in icon painting. He resented the artists' painting "according to their own understanding and not according to sacred tradition: the same subject was treated in various ways, so that although the subjects of several icons might be identical each was painted differently; they no longer abode by the ancient custom of putting an inscription on the icon, and introduced into the painting besides sacred subjects some profane images." One of the icons that aroused Viskovaty's indignation has been preserved up to the present day. It is a complex icon, painted on four panels and representing didactic subjects, which indeed were new in the Russia of that period, although for a long time well known in the Orthodox South and East. As early as the fourteenth and fifteenth centuries we see abstract themes illustrating prayers, dogmas, the liturgy, etc., being treated symbolically and even mystically, but in Moscow they were introduced only during the fifteenth and sixteenth centuries. Their origin can be traced back to the art of the Greek

monasteries, which sought its material in theological treatises and
Latin scholasticism.

Viskovaty's doubts, however, were not of a radical nature, for
like Tsar Ivan he dwelt only on superficial details, and his criticism
was chiefly aimed at annoying Sylvester, the Tsar's favorite and
priest of the Cathedral of the Annunciation. In 1554 an ecclesiastical council succeeded in proving to Viskovaty that his misgivings
were groundless, and caused him to repent having written his
"disparaging lines." Of course the council had reasons for asserting
that the new forms in iconography were not in any way contrary
to tradition. But Viskovaty was right too when, with the trained
eye of a Muscovite, he immediately detected the unusual forms
on the Pskovian icons. God the Father represented in the image
of an elder, and Jesus Christ in the midst of cherubs' wings, which
had annoyed Viskovaty, showed once again the Italian-Greek influence. Moreover, according to Rovinsky, a detail on one of the
new icons painted by two Pskovians for the Cathedral of the Annunciation was copied from a drawing by Cimabue, while another
icon was an exact reproduction of a drawing by Perugino. The
allegorical frescoes upon the walls of the palace were likewise quite
a distinct innovation, but the figure of a "wench dancing with
abandon," intended to represent "Lust," and which particularly
displeased Viskovaty, was in fact the likeness of the dancing
Salome seen in the works of the Italian-Greek school as early as
the fourteenth century.

Indeed, these tendencies towards innovation are no more characteristic of the popular art of icon painting in Russia at the beginning of the sixteenth century than the Italian Kremlin of
Fioravanti, Solario, and Alevisio is of its national architecture.
Innovations were introduced into Moscow by icon painters from
Novgorod and Pskov. In 1547 Metropolitan Macarius ordered all
icon painters to be forcibly brought from these two cities to the
Tsar's capital. That was the time when Moscow, to its own glori-
fication, was collecting Russian Orthodox relics from every part
of the country.[5] This, to a certain extent, especially in the early days,
inevitably led to eclecticism, and mixed styles appeared in Moscow
art. Yet Moscow had its own Suzdal tradition, which was far more

[5] See Part I, ch. 2.—ED.

conservative than that of Novgorod, and it naturally wanted to subordinate the new artists to the old tradition. In 1551, at the Council of Hundred Chapters, the Moscow authorities undertook a number of measures in order to secure Orthodoxy both in art and in ritual. In the forty-third chapter of the Hundred Chapters icon painters were formed into something like a guild subordinate to the ecclesiastical authorities; the prelates of every district were instructed to "insist relentlessly that the expert icon painters and their pupils should copy ancient patterns and not make use of their own ideas and imagination in painting the Divinity: *for we only have the description of Christ our Lord in the flesh, not in His divinity.*" The words italicized have a special interest for us since evidently they are an answer to one of the chief arguments in favor of greater artistic freedom for the icon painters. Apparently, as early as the sixteenth century the followers of the new trend in icon painting were advancing the opinion that they had the right to try and represent the ideal, or spiritual and celestial images of the saints rather than copy their supposed earthly likenesses. But, in the direction of idealization of types, the most they were allowed was to copy Rublev's manner, which in this way was perpetuated throughout the sixteenth century. Any who disregarded the rules were threatened with the Tsar's anger and even with persecution.

The regulations of the Hundred Chapters did not cover all the measures against the new artists' "own ideas," for in the second part of the sixteenth century there appeared the so-called "Illuminated Original," a manual of copies of the established patterns from which the icon painters were obliged to work. To this collection of outline drawings there was added a concise characterization of the types of saints for each day of the year, and a detailed enumeration of the colors necessary for their likeness. The manual was composed for the purpose of establishing types for obligatory use in icon painting, thereby putting an end to the artists' individual inventiveness. However, it failed in attaining this object, for during the seventeenth century the icon painters developed their own ideas to an unprecedented degree. One of the reasons which prevented the "Original" from entirely restricting the independence of the artists was that at the time the manual was composed there no longer existed any uniform types in iconography. The "Orig-

inal" itself provided many variants, the number of which increased
with time. Thus the artist was permitted a relative freedom as
he could choose between different variants. But a still greater
scope for independent work was offered by the complex icons of
the Moscow period.

This type of icon was naturally very popular with the faithful.
In Russia, more than in medieval Europe, the icon had to replace
books; in its conventional, hieratic images it had to relate graphically episodes from the Holy Scriptures, the lives of the saints,
the meaning of holidays; in fact, all that might interest the pious
people in the domain of religion. Thus the icon became the Bible
for the poor. Those who ordered an icon to be painted demanded
the image of a saint "with the story of his life"; the image of Jesus
Christ "with the holidays," and that of the Holy Virgin "with pictures illustrating all the twenty-four verses in Her acathistus." [6]
All these pictures were painted in miniature, framing the central
figure. Of course this type of icon allowed of more or less originality in the composition. The artist still could make no changes in
the established types, but he was permitted a mechanical adjustment of the objects. For this work the Russian icon painters, like
those of all other Orthodox countries, found a wealth of material
in the miniatures of ancient illuminated manuscripts. Obviously,
with this material at their disposal, the artists had wider scope for
their imagination than when merely copying the old compositions.
They were able to introduce new details learned from the Scriptures, sacred songs, or even the Apocrypha, or they could lend to
the mechanical adjustment of parts of the icon a greater spiritual
unity, or at least could group them more artistically on the panel.
This type of icon was the first product of original painting in
Russia to achieve wide popularity.

Moscow icon painting of the sixteenth and seventeenth centuries
forms the last chapter in the history of painting prior to Peter's
time. Modern students regard it as a period of stagnation and decline. While it is impossible to accept this opinion without reservations, it must be admitted that seventeenth-century Moscow was
no longer satisfied to carry on the tradition of the preceding cen-

[6] A special form of prayer used in the Orthodox church to glorify Jesus Christ,
the Virgin, or any particular saint.—Ed.

turies, and that it found itself in an impasse, the only way out of
which was to break with the past. In regard to the past Moscow
had played the part of a centralizing power. It subordinated to
its authority both artists and the artistic styles of Novgorod and
Pskov. From Novgorod the art of icon painting spread throughout the Novgorodian territories in Northwestern Russia, and pre-
sumably was brought from there to the estates of the eminent
Stroganov family, in Ustiug, Solvychegodsk, and Perm, where
during the latter part of the sixteenth and the early seventeenth
centuries their artisans developed it into a style of their own.
The Stroganov icons achieved great renown for the gorgeousness
of their design, the brilliance of color, and the treatment of detail
on their miniatures. The earliest of these artisans, Stephan Arefiev,
is known through the icon he painted in 1596 for Nikita Stroganov.
Even the art of the Stroganov's masters was appropriated by Moscow. Thus Nicephorus Savin worked simultaneously for the
Stroganovs and Tsar Michael. Procopius Chirin, an even better
known artist, left the Stroganovs and entered the service of the
Tsar. In this way the Stroganov style was absorbed by that of
Moscow, and yet Moscow was not satisfied. When the extensive
works of restoring the frescoes in the Cathedral of the Assumption
and that of the Archangel were undertaken (1653, 1657, 1660), the
Tsar issued a strict decree ordering the artists who still remained
in the Northwest to be sent to Moscow, threatening them with
severe punishment in case of disobedience. Those who failed to
escape were brought to Moscow from Kostroma, Ustiug, Vologda,
Ostashkov, Rostov, and other places, in a state of complete desti-
tution. They petitioned the authorities to establish regular relays
and not to summon them too often to Moscow, where a common
artisan received the low wage of from four to seven kopecks a
day.[7] Skilled artisans, however, received steady work and yearly
salaries of from ten to twelve roubles, and became the accredited
icon and picture painters of the Tsar. After the Time of Troubles [8] they were subordinated to the *Oruzheinaia Palata* (Armory

[7] The monetary value in those days exceeded seventeen times that of the pre-
war period [i. e., of the period immediately before 1914 when the value of a
rouble was about fifty cents, and that of a kopeck about half a cent.]—ED.

[8] A period of political and social upheaval in Russia, in the early seventeenth
century.—ED.

Board), which had control of everything relative to the Tsar's household. A number of young people were apprenticed to these artists, and thus towards the second half of the seventeenth century the Moscow school of the "Tsar's isographers" [9] was born.

In depriving the provincial forms of icon painting of their individuality and in subjecting them all to the same influence, the Moscow school helped to establish a uniform eclectic style. The practice of bringing the provincial artisans to work in Moscow and of sending the Muscovite workers to the provinces facilitated this unification.

The real value of the Moscow school, however, was neither in this process of unification nor in the development of ancient motifs, but in its effort to meet the demands of the moment. The achievements to be attained through copying of patterns, including those of Rublev, were exhausted, but new ideas came to Moscow from Byzantium, the Italian-Greek schools, and, in a far more developed form, directly from the West. Foreign artists were attached even to the Tsar's school, not for religious, it is true, but for secular painting. The importance and value bestowed upon them can be seen in the fact that their salaries far exceeded those of the best Russian masters. Thus, after thirty years of service the famous Simon Ushakov received sixty-seven roubles a year while Antz Detters, a foreigner, was paid two hundred and fifty. The palaces of Tsar Alexis in Moscow and Kolomenskoe abounded in foreign works, but supervision over their decoration and repairs was nevertheless entrusted to Simon Ushakov. The introduction of foreign engravings also helped to extend the influence of Western art, which became known under the collective name of *Friaz*.[10] During the sixteenth century it was chiefly German, but towards the middle of the seventeenth century Netherland-Flemish influence also reached the country. Having easily conquered both decorative art and portraiture, *Friaz* soon spread to icon painting as well. In his day Patriarch Nikon, who patronized Greek innovations, had already noticed the Latin influence in some of the icons, and became very

[9] According to Kondakov, the term "isographer" was used to designate a "real creative painter," and not a mere "skilled practitioner." In some cases, however, it seems to have been synonymous with "iconographer."—Ed.

[10] Apparently a modification of "Frankish."—Ed.

indignant. With a characteristic display of temperament he threw these icons on the stone floor of the church, pierced the eyes of the saints, and disregarding the pleas of the Tsar ordered them burned, while he called out the names of their owners. To justify his iconoclasm Nikon afterwards told the people of Moscow that the style of the destroyed icons was "imported by Germans from the German land." It is clear that Nikon was attacking what to him was a new and dangerous departure in icon painting. The same position was taken by his opponent Avvakum [11] who, in one of his epistles, expressed himself as follows:

With the Lord's sufferance, the number of painters using an unseemly manner of icon painting has increased in our land. They paint the image of the Saviour Emmanuel with bloated face, red lips, swollen fingers, and large, fat legs and thighs, His whole figure that of a German, fat-bellied and corpulent, only omitting to paint a sword at His side. It was the fiend Nikon's idea that paintings should be true to life; he contrived that everything should be in the *Friaz,* or German manner.

This charge against Nikon was indeed unjust, for in addition to burning the icons he solemnly denounced the new trend in painting from the pulpit and, in the presence of the Eastern Patriarch, pronounced anathema upon its followers. The Church Council of 1667 likewise condemned the adaptation of Western methods in iconography. But none of these denunciations or interdictions bore any practical results. All the church was able to achieve was that ancient methods, prescribed by the old "Original," were used in painting icons for its official needs. This did not prevent the pictorial manner from gaining power in the field of religious painting, for even the most renowned masters, such as Simon Ushakov, began to work in both manners simultaneously, depending on the taste of their patrons. We have already seen that from the time of Tsar Michael there appeared at the court of Moscow some foreign artists, Poles and Germans, who entered the Tsar's service and were commissioned to paint both pictures and portraits. After the forties of the seventeenth century there was a continuous influx of them into Russia where they had many Russian pupils. It

[11] On Nikon and Avvakum, see Part I, ch. 3.—Ed.

was but natural that, having received an adequate training and being encouraged by commissions from the Tsar, the Muscovite artists of the Tsar's school resolutely introduced *Friaz* methods into the art of icon painting, and even assumed an offensive instead of the former defensive attitude.

One day Joseph Vladimirov, an isographer, was sitting in the workroom of his friend Simon Ushakov discussing art, when John Pleshkovich, a Serbian archdeacon, entered and joined in their conversation. On seeing a picture of Mary Magdalen, Pleshkovich spat and said that images like that were not acceptable. In the form of an epistle to Ushakov, Joseph wrote a vigorous retort: "Canst thou possibly say," he questioned his opponent Pleshkovich,

that only Russians are capable of painting icons, that only icons of Russian painting should be worshiped, and that those of other lands should neither be accepted nor honored? Ask thy father or the elders, and they will tell thee that in all our Christian-Russian churches the church plate, chasubles, omophoria, altar cloths and palls, ornamental and gold cloths, precious stones and pearls—all these thou receivest from the foreigners and bringest them into church to adorn the altar and icons with no thought of their being good or bad. . . . Thou demandest that in our days the painter paint lugubrious and ungainly images and thus teachest us that we should be false to the ancient Scriptures. . . . Where and who found the instruction about painting the faces of the saints in dark, swarthy shades? Was the countenance of all mankind created alike? Were all the saints dark and gaunt? Even had they mortified their flesh here on earth, in heaven their souls and bodies would appear revived and radiant. What devil, being envious of the truth, plotted against the radiant persons of the saints? Who among reasonable people would not laugh at the folly that prefers darkness and gloom to light? No, this is not the idea of a wise artist. He outlines in forms and faces what he sees or hears, and in accordance with his seeing and hearing he pictures them. And as in the Old Testament so in the New have many saints, both male and female, appeared comely.

The idea that pictorial icons could lead to temptation aroused the pious artist's indignation. "Art thou then, unworthy one," he exclaims, "not afraid to look at the blissful faces with temptation in thy heart? A true and pious Christian should not be tempted even though he look at harlots, so how could he be inflamed by a beautiful painting. To think that one can be tempted by an icon is impiety and brazenness. Only those ruled by flesh and not by spirit could in their foolishness conceive such an idea; they are blinded by wickedness."

Thus the realistic artists of the late seventeenth century retained the same fundamental premises as the idealistic icon painters of the fifteenth. They shared the exalted Christian ideas of their predecessors, and were unable to conceive that naturalism in painting could overstep the limits permitted by religion.

This exalted mood of the Russian artists of the period supplies the key to a proper understanding of some new and interesting phenomena in the iconography of the late seventeenth century. This time the matter reached beyond the mere addition of details to old compositions or the mechanical readjustment of old motifs in order to represent new subjects. The change was now introduced into the conception of composition itself, and every Christian artist strove to lift it up to the level of his own religious emotions. Thus the ancient composition of the Annunciation, representing the Holy Virgin sitting by a well or house and spinning, no longer satisfied the Russian artist, and he pictured her reading the Holy Scriptures. Dmitry of Rostov, a Russian prelate, has given us a clear explanation of this change. "The Archangel had to find the Holy Virgin," he says, "not outside the house, not in the midst of everyday duties, but absorbed in prayer, meditation, and reading." The artist was equally provoked at the reclining position given the Holy Virgin on the Byzantine icons of the Nativity, seeing in it a suggestion of human weakness, so he painted her seated, thus unwittingly restoring the position she was given in early Christian art. This time it is the artist himself who gives us his reason for the change by saying that "only crude and ignorant icon painters could represent the Divine Mother in the image of an earthly woman, lying down and attended by a midwife: unaided She gave birth to the Child, wrapped Him in swaddling clothes, reverently embraced and kissed Him, and gave Him the breast. There was no pain, no weakness in childbirth, only joy." Following the promptings of the same religious feeling the manger where Christ was born was replaced by a grotto.

A peculiarity characteristic of the increasing Western influence
in icon and fresco painting during the seventeenth century was
that the artist mastered the subject of the "interior," that is to say
the inside of the house, and began to paint it instead of a mono-
chrome background as on the old icons. Although at first the
rooms had no connection with the figures and were painted in one
plane, like a stage setting, the fact of their introduction was a sign
of progress in the history of religious painting. At the end of the
seventeenth century the Russian artists first brought forward the
side walls of the chamber to surround the figure, and then opened
the façade presenting a vista of rooms. Thus flat drawing was replaced by a plane of three dimensions, giving the picture a more
realistic character. Yet it must be said that almost the entire process
of conquering the interior took place without the artist's knowledge of the cardinal rules of perspective. In the West the problem
was successfully solved by Giotto and his contemporaries as early
as the end of the thirteenth and the beginning of the fourteenth
centuries, and at that with knowledge of perspective. In Russia,
however, the final victory of the new school was attained only
during the last quarter of the seventeenth century, and then perspective was still ignored, for even in the "Siisk Illuminated Original," completed in 1666–76, no such achievement is to be seen.
But we have evidence to show that immediately thereafter a
new and strong foreign influence manifested itself in Russia. It
emanated from a well-known source, the so-called "Bible of Piscator," [12] and was recorded by the frescoes in the churches of
Iaroslavl, Kostroma, Rostov, Vologda, and other towns of Northern Russia. One much-thumbed copy of the Bible of Piscator was
even found in Vologda, while we know that another copy (probably the Amsterdam edition either of 1650 or 1674) had been acquired in 1677 by Bezmin, one of the Tsar's artists, for the personal
use of Tsar Theodore. When it reached Russia the Bible of Piscator was one hundred years behind the times, for it reproduced
chiefly the works of the sixteenth-century masters. Through this
medium the Italian influence came to Russia as reflected in the

---

[12] Johannes Piscator (Johann Fischer) published a German version of the
Bible in the early seventeenth century. Here the reference is to the illustrated editions of this work.—ED.

prism of the Netherlands Gothic Baroque. But this art was already quite familiar with the rules of linear and aerial perspective.

The new school of icon painting revised all the iconographic material, compared all the established types with the text of the Scriptures, and, where possible, introduced spontaneous feeling and vitality instead of the dry Byzantine formalism. This resulted in the appearance of the so-called "Critical Original," which supplied the artists with themes taken directly from church literature, thus liberating them from routine icon painting. Moreover, in destroying the old tradition, the adherents of the new trend endeavored to create another one, and to this end collected the best modern and most outstanding old patterns as well as some entirely independent compositions to serve as a manual for future icon painters (Siisk Illuminated Original). It is important to mention that the favorite subjects for new religious paintings were actually the same as those of the book most popular with the pious people of that period. In the last quarter of the seventeenth century there appeared the illustrated *Passions of the Lord,* which received such a wide circulation that the subject was immediately chosen for the frescoes in the Tsar's chambers. Apparently it was also at that time that a detailed treatment of the infernal torments was added to the traditional representation of the Last Judgment.

It seems that Russian art, living in the atmosphere of general religious exaltation, stood at that moment on the threshold of another revival of Christian painting, similar to the one experienced in the West during the fourteenth and fifteenth centuries. Had it been left to its own devices, Russian art perhaps could have followed the same path as that of Western art, and three or four centuries later would have attained its classical epoch. But because of the religious conditions in Russia at the beginning of the eighteenth century such development was made impossible. The majority of the faithful in the Russia of those days firmly upheld church antiquity and had no wish to support iconographic innovations, while those who advocated church reforms were not concerned with the problems of art. As to the rest of the people, they were soon totally unable to grasp the spirit that guided the Christian artist. Thus the cause of the modest movement, begun in the workrooms of the Tsar's icon painters in Moscow, was lost before it had had time to develop its new tendencies. The inspiration of these artists could not appeal to anyone, and their work was no longer wanted. In a few decades the influential groups of Russian society had skipped over centuries of Western progress and now were anxious to keep up with its very latest phase. But, as we know, by that time Western art had long since outlived its period of youthful and naïve inspiration. Having mastered all the secrets of the technique and having achieved classical perfection, it became satiated and thus succumbed to mannerism. In trying to imitate the contemporary Western patterns, Russian art interrupted the course of its original development, abandoned the difficult, faltering attempts to feel its own way, and meekly surrendered itself as apprentice to Western masters.

The social system, which the Russian artist was made to serve, also led him along the same path of mechanical imitation. In the great majority of cases the Russian artists of the period were hirelings or even serfs, who were never asked what God they really worshiped in their hearts. At an early age, when their individual leanings had not yet been formed, they were usually sent to study with some good master, who was paid well for their instruction. Thereafter they were required to work absolutely in the same manner and as well, if not better, than the master, or their work was not accepted. The art of painting, like architecture, was subordinated to the demands of the rich, and for a long time in both fields the state, as chief patron, not only laid down the law of taste, but also directed the instruction in art at the Academy, which had been entrusted to foreigners.

Under these conditions, as we know, the taste for Baroque, Rococo, and both Roman and Greek forms of classicism that prevailed in Western Europe in turn triumphed in Russian architecture. In its essence the art of painting is closer to that of letters than to architecture, and here we are at once surrounded by the atmosphere familiar to us through the history of literature. The Academy introduced into painting the same pseudo-classicism mingled with sentimentalism that prevailed in the literature of that time.[13] Painters too developed their own "exalted" and "common" styles, for fashion demanded that they, like the writers, should express

[13] For the parallel development in literature, see Part II, ch. 1.—ED.

themselves in the conventional language of "ideal" art. The exalted style was represented by religious and historical subjects painted in a conventional, "purified" manner, with its set types, attitudes, gestures, and drapery, its disdain for landscape, great preference for nude, and a complete system of restrictions, which excluded painting true to life. Those aspiring to receive a degree from the Academy or orders from noble patrons had to choose their themes from the Old and the New Testament, or from Greek and Roman mythology and history, and only the most daring ventured to paint episodes from ancient Russian history or battle scenes of the more recent period depicting the heroic deeds of the national sovereigns. The common style of painting representing everyday life was the genre, but this was never taken very seriously, and was only tolerated on the condition that the artist comply with the conventional rules. Immortality and fame were as unattainable to the genre painters as in literature they were to the prose writer, and only those who practised exalted art were considered to possess true artistic talent.

Some branches of painting, however, and precisely those not patronized by the state and the Academy, were so closely related to life that in them the exigencies of realistic representation were soon to break through the defense of academic conventionality. In these cases the subjects chosen were familiar to everybody, and even the rich patrons demanded a likeness of the model and consequently a realistic treatment. The earliest efforts at original work, more or less independent of Western influence, were manifested in landscape and portrait painting. These early creative efforts modified the general opinion on the imitative period in Russian art. One must agree with Buslaev that

. . . no matter how artificially the cultured society of Russia had molded itself, nor in what haphazard way the academic school of painting had been created, no one could possibly deny the merits of young Russian art, which had so quickly mastered foreign technique and thus had learned to render the various shades of unfamiliar emotions and thoughts that drifted into Russia from Western culture.

It is true that the distinguished patrons for a long time did not appreciate landscape for its own sake, but they were naturally interested in recording on canvas the magnificent buildings and French "perspective" gardens which they had erected and planned. Thus the first task of a landscape painter was a purely topographical one, for he had either to represent accurately in "perspective painting," as Peter the Great had called it, panoramas of streets, palaces, and country manors, or record the designs made for the elaborate transparencies used for the display of fireworks on solemn occasions. The art of engraving was of great assistance in the performance of this task.

By its very nature an engraving was always more within the reach of the masses than a painting. In Russia it had been popular from early times in the form of a primitive woodcut (*lubok*). Even during the late part of the seventeenth century the *Friaz* plates, that is, foreign engravings, could be bought in Moscow at a very low price. Peter the Great learned to engrave "with a style and aquatint under the guidance of Adrian Schoonebeck of Amsterdam," reads the inscription on an etching done by him and dated 1698. Since his time the art of engraving has prospered in St. Petersburg. "Illuminated News about Monsters," "Illuminated Announcement of Military Campaigns," and the like, replaced newspapers for the masses, while numerous etchings, sold at popular prices, reproduced all the favorite themes of Russian folklore. The art of engraving was used also to popularize the new architecture. Several young Russians studied engraving with Schoonebeck, and one of them, Zubov, made etchings of buildings erected by Peter I in St. Petersburg. It was during the reign of this monarch that Wortmann came to Russia and taught the engraving of portraits until 1745, when he ceded his place to his best pupil Ivan Sokolov, the "master of portrait etching," who had made the illustrations for the *Description of the Coronation of the Empress Elizabeth*. Makhaev, the "master of maps and perspective painting," was the most outstanding of Sokolov's pupils, and is known through series of views he engraved of St. Petersburg. Schmidt, the third foreign engraver, headed that art in Russia during the second half of the eighteenth century, and when he left the country his tradition was upheld by Chemesov, who was considered most gifted among his pupils. It was due no doubt to the popularity of etchings that both landscape and portrait painting gradually became emancipated from academic rules.

Of the two, the portrait painting of the eighteenth century occupies, of course, the foremost position. Peter the Great not only invited the foreign portrait painters Tannauer and Caravaque to come to Russia, but also sent some of his young artists to study this particular branch of art abroad. Andrew Matveiev and I. Nikitin, two of the students, were rather successful. Caravaque found that Matveiev was abler in the use of colors than in drawing, and this proved to be prophetic of the great part color was to play in Russian painting. It was Matveiev who drew the sketches for the murals in the SS. Peter and Paul Cathedral, while Nikitin, having finished his studies in Italy and France, was appointed "master of personal art" and taught the engravers to work from life models.

The art of painting, like that of architecture, was given a new and final impetus by the establishment of the Academy and the arrival of new artists from abroad. We see the outstanding masters, such as Count Rotari, Torelli, de Wailly, Tocqué, Le Lorrain, and Lagrenée, whom Empress Elizabeth had invited to work on the murals in the palaces and who also painted portraits, being joined in the reign of Catherine II by another score of artists, mostly German, of whom Christineck and Ritt were the most outstanding, and somewhat later by Lampi, Roslin, Ericsson, and Mme Vigée-Lebrun. Many of these artists exerted either a direct or indirect influence over their Russian pupils. Towards the end of the eighteenth century Russia already had artists of her own who were equal to their foreign masters. Among the older generation there were Antropov, the son of a soldier, who imitated Rotari's famous pictures of feminine heads, the Argunov brothers, who were Count Sheremetev's serfs, and Rokotov, a follower of Le Lorrain, Rotari, and Tocqué, whose success was so great that he scarcely had time to execute all the portraits ordered. In the ranks of the younger generation, taught already by Russian masters, there appeared such famous names as Levitsky, a pupil of Antropov; Losenko, a pupil of Ivan Argunov; and Borovikovsky, who had studied under Losenko and Lampi.

The most famous of these, Levitsky and Borovikovsky, created a school of their own, thereby establishing a Russian tradition. In the field of exalted art, when painting historical or emblematic subjects, these artists had to remain under the sway of the Academy, but in common art, which included portrait, landscape, and especially genre painting, they succeeded in emancipating themselves from the influence of the Academy's plaster and model classes, and by drawing nearer to the life model they created many remarkable works. Levitsky, a Ukrainian (1735–1822), painted coquettish noblewomen and portrayed society in a light-hearted spirit. The experts liken him to Gainsborough, though of course the famous Englishman had greater depth of feeling. There was more monotony in Borovikovsky's (1757–1825) dreamy, languid, and pale feminine types, but he was a greater master of color. Losenko was distinguished for the precision of his drawing. Kiprensky (1783–1836), whose activity belongs to the reign of Alexander I, was known for his turbulent nature and great susceptibility to feminine beauty. In his works we find amply reflected the strains of sensibility and romanticism. The latter, however, was only a passing influence, but tribute was paid to sensibility even in the days of Catherine II by abandoning the straight lines of French gardens and replacing them with the "curves, soft slopes, and ponds" of the English. That was also the period when, under the influence of Rousseau, there appeared in the parks of the noblemen's estates a profusion of "hermitages," pavilions of "friendship" and "seclusion," rustic farms, and cottages fashioned after those of the Trianon. The critics unanimously agree that Kiprensky ruined his talent by spending the last twenty years of his life in Rome, where he was infected with the germ of academism which he had escaped in St. Petersburg. The trend of emotionalism, though without Kiprensky's turbulent romanticism, was sustained in Moscow by Tropinin (1786–1857), also born a serf. Tropinin's "Seamstress" and "Lacemaker," notwithstanding their mannered sweetness, foreshadowed the future victory of the realistic genre.

At the end of the eighteenth and the beginning of the nineteenth centuries realism also found its way into the field of landscape painting. Both Michael Ivanov, a pupil of Le Prince, and Theodore Alekseiev, a pupil of Belotto (surnamed Caneletto), ventured to overstep the confines of strict "perspectivism." They were followed by Galaktionov and Martynov, two "poets of St. Petersburg," and Vorobiev, the dreamy artist of St. Petersburg's sunrise, sunset, and moonlight. At an early age Vorobiev left Russia to seek beauty abroad and was joined there by Sylvester Shchedrin, the most gifted landscape painter of that time, who fell in love with Sorrento and remained there until his last days.

More significant, however, was the development in the field of genre which being the most "common" form of art, naturally tended towards the greatest deviation from the academic style. Indeed, to paint life as it could be observed every day seemed a strange notion not worthy of art. Reality had to pass through the prism of academic training and emerge from it ennobled. Characteristically, the first representative of genre and caricature was A. O. Orlovsky (1777–1832), a Russianized Pole and son of a common innkeeper, who made his way into high society. Orlovsky was an eccentric, he worked not only with the brush, but with the point of a match, a candle wick, or with his fingers and his nose dipped in ink. With these devices he drew caricatures, costumes for fancy dress balls, and comic scenes of popular life. He was very prolific and left to posterity a great number of sketches drawn in pen, pastels, charcoal, and pencil, some of them absurd and some extremely lifelike and clever. About that time (1815), a new method for reproducing drawings by lithography had just been invented, and thus copies of Orlovsky's works were circulated in great number. They represented a variety of subjects including peasants and merchants, cadets and generals, Kalmucks and Tatars, thoroughbred horses and work horses.

Apart from this striking example of deviation from accepted artistic standards, one could mention a few other names of artists who tried to imitate Le Prince in genre painting. Even at the Academy there was a special class in which pupils had to paint such subjects as "a bourgeois having a slight seizure and preparing to take medicine," but this type of work was never considered important. A picture bearing the signature of Losenko and dated 1757, in which an artist was represented in his studio painting the portrait of a child, was so unusual for those days that it aroused suspicion as to its authenticity and date (its true author, in fact, was Ivan Fedorov). Half a century elapsed before a Muscovite, Alexis Venetsianov (1780–1847), the true father of genre in Russia, appeared in St. Petersburg. Venetsianov had great admiration for the Dutch school and had repeatedly attempted to paint from life, but it was a picture by Granet, exhibited in 1820 at the Hermitage, that determined for him his vocation. "This picture," he said, "helped us greatly to understand the art of painting. We began to see in art quite a new quality which up to that time had never been noticed. We saw objects painted not only with likeness and accuracy but full of life; not just a painting from life but life itself on a canvas." Venetsianov further explained why the picture produced such an impression.

It was said that its fascination was created by the focus of light . . . that with full light it is quite impossible to paint objects with such forceful vitality. But I decided to overcome the impossible, went to the country and set to work. In order to succeed I departed from all the rules and methods learned by me during the twelve years of copying at the Hermitage, and then in the most natural way Granet's methods were revealed to me. The idea was that nothing should be represented except as it appears in nature: to follow its dictates and not to mix with it the methods of any painter, that is not to paint á la Rembrandt or á la Rubens, but simply, so to speak, á la nature.

As we see it, the task was defined with a precision quite extraordinary for those days. Not only was Venetsianov in advance of the Russian realists of the eighteen sixties and seventies, but even of such French *pleinairists* as Monet and others. No less remarkable was the systematic manner in which he set about to realize his plans. Venetsianov resigned his position as geodesist, bought a small place in the country, and after spending three years there in complete seclusion finally in 1824 presented the Emperor with his picture "The Barn." In order to have full light in a dark place, he removed the entire front wall and thus lighted the foreground of the deep shed where he painted peasants threshing grain. This radical method of obtaining full light, that is, to paint in the open instead of a studio, was also employed by other Russian artists. Krylov, a pupil of Venetsianov, in painting a winter landscape worked in a hut which he built in the middle of a field. F. Tolstoy, Reutern, and Zelenko followed in Venetsianov's footsteps and mastered the subject of lighted interiors, vistas of rooms, studios, etc. Yet the conventionalities of the time were reflected in the works of the master and his pupils. Venetsianov's figures are not natural, they pose in frozen attitudes, and his peasants remind one of the rustics on the stage of those days. The artist seems ashamed to present them to the public unwashed and uncombed, and so first teaches them good manners and attires them in Sunday clothes. And yet for his time Venetsianov was an astounding realist, and the prematureness of his art was emphasized by the fact that while he remained in the background occupied with the solution of new problems in genre, academism gained in strength and celebrated its victories boisterously in the works of Bruellow and Bruni.

The opinionated and vainglorious Karl Bruellow (1799–1852), who from early youth had always aspired to become a great artist, upheld the honor of the Academy and infused its style with artificial life. After a protracted training in Rome and eleven months of assiduous work, Bruellow exhibited his canvas "The Last Day of Pompeii," which had the pretense of genius and was widely advertised. The rumors about Bruellow's triumph abroad had preceded the appearance of his work in St. Petersburg, where it was finally placed on view, first at the Winter Palace, and then at the Academy of Arts. Purely academic in treatment, it was introduced to the public under the banner of Romanticism, and for the first time in Russia the success of a painting became a social event. "The Last Day of Pompeii" was abundant with life as compared with the "gentle boredom and icy immobility" that reigned in the works of the Russians who imitated Mengs and David. People fleeing, falling buildings, all under the bright glow of eruption and conflagration, the lavishness of color, the movement of figures, the effects of light and the expression of terror and despair in Bruellow's picture produced as deep an impression upon the Russian public as fifteen years previously the French people felt when they saw "The Raft of the Frigate Medusa," that famous work of Géricault, the herald of Romanticism in the art of painting. The impression in Russia was even more profound, because it was the first experienced, and while it may not have been justified, the fact that it actually had a lasting effect cannot be denied. One should remember that during the middle thirties of the nineteenth century Romanticism was a passion with the Russian intelligentsia.

Thus the first strong impression produced by a work of art upon the Russian public was at the same time the first victory over the conventionalities of academic classicism. Of course such victory could be only of a temporary nature. That which, compared to the preceding period of stagnation in art, had for a moment appeared true to life presently proved to be ostentatious and rhetorical. In their separate rôles the characters in "The Last Day of Pompeii" were too frankly posing before the audience, and the whole scene suggested too vividly the premeditated and studied effects of a stage performance. Clearly Bruellow's position in the history of Russian art was only an intermediate and passing one. He was the Derzhavin of Russian painting,[14] and like that poet he strove only to instill life into the antiquated classical forms without changing them, and by adhering to this cause he soon became as obsolete as the forms themselves. He intended with his second large canvas, "The Siege of Pskov," to lay the foundation for a national art; but this labored and artificial production made very little impression, and Bruellow retained his renown only because of his remarkable portraits. However, the incentive he gave to artists and the public was not in vain, although in each instance the interest aroused was soon directed in an absolutely different channel.

In the same year that Bruellow's "The Last Day of Pompeii" was achieving enormous success in St. Petersburg, Alexander Ivanov (b. 1806) started a canvas [15] in Rome hoping that it would create the revolution in Russian art which Bruellow's work had failed to produce. Ivanov deliberately set out to abolish the old academic trend and introduce both truth and life into painting, but this attempt also failed and now it only has an historical interest. He had worked on his canvas for such a long time that when it was finished, it proved to be behind the needs of the moment. In fact, its fate gives us the best proof of the rapid progress achieved both

[14] The comparison is with the famous poet of the eighteenth century. See Part II, ch. 1.—Ed.

[15] "Christ Appears to the People."—Ed.

by the Russian artists and the public during this period. In the twenties of the nineteenth century, when the painting was first conceived, seeking for truth and local color was a great novelty. These ambitions were still unusual even twelve years later when Ivanov actually started to work on his canvas (1836). But when after another twelve years (1848) his work was finished, the artist was to discover that in the meantime his surroundings had completely altered. Indeed, Ivanov himself underwent a change, for he lost his religious idealism and came to the definite conclusion that he had wasted his life on work that was worthless to Russian society, which required something quite different. With his characteristic honesty he then zealously sought that "something different," but up to the last he never succeeded either in escaping the vicious circle of the academic desert or in obtaining even a distant glimpse of the promised land of national art. As he died only a few weeks after his return to Russia from Italy (1858), Ivanov was not able to learn that the principle of national art which he sought so long and never attained was there within his reach, ripening and forcing its way into the world, though not in the form of religious painting.

In the meantime genre, the prose of painting, its social novel and story, had long since taken roots in Russia, and towards the middle of the century its first shoots were visible. Venetsianov was the Karamzin of Russian painting [16] because like that writer he also knew how to adorn the real life of Russia with proper forms, very much polished and sweetened, in order to make the subject acceptable to contemporary art. No one could be shocked by the good peasants and virtuous landowners of Venetsianov's genre, and even the Academy deigned to extend its patronage to this "agreeable type of painting." But in 1848 the indecent behavior of the genre introduced violent discord in the peaceful cohabitation of the two styles and forever spoiled their relationship. At the Academy's annual exhibition Fedotov (1815–52) showed his famous canvas entitled "The Morning of a Bureaucrat upon Receiving His First Decoration," which for the sake of precaution was unassumingly listed in the catalogue as "The Result of a

[16] On Karamzin, the greatest representative of Sentimentalism in Russian literature, see Part II, chs. 1 and 2.—ED.

Carousal." The precaution was wise because when it came to re-producing the picture in lithograph it was necessary to take even further measures and remove the decoration from the dressing gown of the newly created knight. The reason for these precautionary measures was clear to all: Russian painting for the first time had dared to portray reality as honestly and unadorned as it was described in literature by Gogol. In 1849 Fedotov exhibited another great work, "The Major's Courting," which he treated in the spirit of the dramatist Ostrovsky, then rising to fame.[17] Russian art could now celebrate its majority.

The public acclaimed Fedotov, but the world of art, where, until the end of the reign of Nicholas I, Bruellow continued to rule, met his achievements with contempt and criticism. Fedotov had never had the slightest premonition that his works were to be the fore-runners of a great movement which began with the accession to the throne of Alexander II and led to the establishment of an independent Russian school of painting.

Art had now finally overtaken literature, and in its further development from this time on it relied on the latter. The yearning of Russian artists for truth and reality merely duplicated the mood then current in literature, and artists and writers joined in the struggle against the common enemy—the hated old tradition. In the world of art, as everywhere else, the old authorities had to be definitely overthrown. V. V. Stasov, the critic, who in 1852–56 still believed in Bruellow's genius, became thoroughly disillusioned by 1861 and began to criticize severely the artist's methods. The same work which in its wealth of artistic imagination he had recently regarded as almost immortal, Stasov now considered as insulting to the dignity of man. Under such conditions it was quite natural that Ivanov's painting, which had stood in the studio for ten years after it was finished and was condemned by the artist himself, failed to receive recognition when exhibited in 1858. By that time the young artists were anxious to break all bonds with the past, the Academy, and exalted art.

[17] On Gogol and Ostrovsky, see Part II, ch. 2.—ED.

III

PAINTING: SINCE THE MIDDLE OF THE

NINETEENTH CENTURY

THE critical moment in both art and literature coincided with the beginning of Alexander II's reign (1855). Both experienced the influence of that general spirit of liberty which at the time was animating Russian society. It manifested itself negatively in the protest against all officially approved standards, and positively in the acceptance by the artists of the idea of serving the people. The principles of realism established during the preceding epoch now gained in strength and growth. But in harmony with the general mood which prevailed during the first decade of the new reign, realism in art was made to serve a utilitarian task—that of exposing the evils of the existing order. By this it disclosed both its newly acquired strength and its temporary weakness, inasmuch as the utilitarian approach was inconsistent with art's proper function—artistic realism.

The crisis which took place in the field of painting was due to two specific circumstances. First, during the eighteen-forties the Academy of Arts ceased to be a boarding school as it had been previously, so that the students were turned out into the streets from the Academy "greenhouses." This change brought rapid results. The well-mannered, respectful academic youths, who were taught to obey the authorities and to strive to please the taste of socially prominent patrons, soon became artistic bohemians. New trends of art could more easily find their way into that emancipated set because now it had a distinct sense of independence which made it receptive to innovations. The other circumstance that

weakened the influence of the Academy was the establishment in
Moscow of a rival institution, the School of Painting, Sculpture,
and Architecture.

Moscow art had always aspired to be independent of St.
Petersburg. The Moscow school, though officially patronized by
the Academy, was too remote to be really influenced by the latter,
and consequently there developed a much greater freedom in its
methods of teaching. In the late eighteen-fifties there appeared in
Moscow a new trend among the artists who even dreamed of
inculcating the spirit of liberty into the Academy itself. It should
be mentioned also that precisely at this time there lived in Moscow
the cultured Maecenas, S. M. Tretiakov, who by his generous pur-
chases, which formed the nucleus for the famous Tretiakov Art
Gallery, provided the material basis for the activity of the young
artists.

In 1863 the mood of the young generation of artists found characteristic expression when thirteen talented pupils of the Academy
refused to accept "Odin in Valhalla" as the official theme in the
contest for the gold medal. They decided that academic training
and scholarship abroad were no longer necessary, avoided with
horror imitating the great works of the old masters, and sought
their inspiration directly in nature and life, preferably of their
native land. Having forsaken the Academy the youths formed
their own guild (artel), which subsequently became the nucleus
of the Fellowship of Itinerant Exhibitions. For a group that was
averse to hypocrisy and learned pedantry, that declared war on
conventionality and wanted to be universally understood, the
most natural issue was an appeal to the public. Soon the atmosphere of the academic exhibitions became too confined for the
members of the new group and in 1871 they opened their first
Itinerant Exhibition, which at once won the interest of the public.

This movement of the eighteen-sixties developed into a growing
success. Perov (1832–82), who may be called the Nekrasov of
Russian painting,[1] was followed by a host of talented artists who
transferred to canvas all the actuality of Russian life. Town and
country, capital cities and remote provincial corners; all classes

[1] On Nekrasov, the greatest civic poet of the period, see Part II, ch. 2.—ED.

of society—peasants, commoners, landowners, clergy; people of every profession—officials, traders, doctors, lawyers, university students; every condition of life—work, political exile, crime, heroic deeds, and peaceful family relations; the entire gamut of emotions, from a trivial joke to a tragedy of horror; in a word, all the manifold aspects of everyday life immediately became the subjects for painting, and genre, which lately had occupied a secondary position, now monopolized public attention. Religious subjects were no longer able to inspire the artists, and they seldom succeeded in creating good historical pictures, but when they could stand on the firm ground of reality, where their art had to be true to life, they usually achieved brilliant success. Like the literature of the period, the new art was accused of being biased, of having a tendency to expose the social evils, and of having developed realism to the point of exaggeration and caricature. The facts that provoked these accusations cannot be denied nor need we exonerate them, for in this instance art merely expressed the actual mood of contemporary society. Indeed the principle of realism was far broader and more deeply rooted in the evolution of Russian art than was at first apparent. Withdrawn as it was from tradition and schooling during the initial stage of its development, the new Russian art was bound to be spontaneous and antagonistic to everything that was artificial. When the eagerness for exposing social evils subsided, art ceased to be sententious but retained its instructive and realistic character.

Thus Perov was followed by Repin (1844–1930) who, without any sentimentality or animosity, gave to Russian art a far greater power of expression than did all Perov's youthful invectives. In order to arouse in the public a critical attitude towards the village priest it was not necessary for Repin to represent him at the moment of utter abasement. On the contrary, he could paint a religious procession, typical of the official church in all its glory, and produce thereby a far deeper and more lasting impression. In his "Burlaky" (the Volga boatmen), out of the ragged crowd of men Repin created an artistic symbol of Russian people who for centuries had carried the heavy burden of obligations imposed upon them by the state. And, of course, this genre will become no less an historical painting than his "Zaporozhtsy" (seventeenth-century Ukrainian Cossacks), which represents a group of tramps, who finding no room within the limits of the organized statehood, formed themselves into a devil-may-care Cossack "Knighthood." As we see, everything was within the power of Repin's realism, even the broadest historical conceptions, and only in the field of religious subjects did he prove impotent, for his "St. Nicholas" was just another historical canvas. But this was because neither the epoch nor the prevailing mood was propitious to religious painting. Had the national school of painting been founded in Russia during the end of the seventeenth century, it would have developed along the lines of religious art of the pre-Raphael period; in the second half of the nineteenth century it could only achieve its progress on the basis of social struggle and everyday life.

However, the period in the history of Russian art which we have just described was not destined to be the final one. Corresponding to the classical period of Russian literature,[2] it shared the latter's fate. Realism in art, as represented by the Itinerants, made its appearance considerably later than in literature, yet both ended almost simultaneously, in the eighteen-eighties and nineties, and under the same pressure from the new generation. The new break with tradition and the revolt of youth during the nineties were, in a sense, a replica of that of the Itinerants against the Academists. But while the earlier revolt had aimed at the creation of a national Russian school of art, the new one took up the banner of cosmopolitanism. Even more vividly than in literature, though with the same delay, every modern Western tendency was reflected in the new school of painting. In both cases Western influence led Russian genius away from realism, and thus to the loss of power over the masses which can be exercised only by realistic art.

The new generation of artists and art critics rallied around the *World of Art,* a periodical published between 1898 and 1902. Perhaps the best way of studying the positive views of this group is through analyzing its repudiations. The World of Art denied first of all academism, in which it saw nothing but conventionality and insincerity, "traits characteristic of academism of every period," but intensified in Russia by the academicians' neglect of modern

[2] See Part II, ch. 2.—Ed.

Western art. Yet the group was equally vigorous in repudiating the tendentious art of the Itinerants, and in general all the realistic and positivist ideas which had been so popular with the preceding generation. In the opinion of the new school, the simplest way to cause a revolution in Russian art was to bring it into closer contact with that of the West. According to Benois, one of the leaders of the World of Art group,

. . . in the seventies and even in the eighties there was no connection between us [the Russian painters] and the truly creative art in the West. . . . We . . . knew only the official artists, such boring academicians as Bouguereau, Cabanel, Gérôme, and Piloty, or the "sugary" salon artists, like Makart, Zihel, Lefebvre, and a few amusing raconteurs. It was only about eight years ago that the English pre-Raphaelites were first mentioned here; Boecklin, Menzel, Whistler, and Leibl were quite unknown, while Millet, Corot, and the Impressionists were regarded as charlatans raised to high rank by the art dealers of Paris. But during the last ten years conditions have changed very rapidly. Thanks to frequent exhibitions of the works of Western artists in St. Petersburg and Moscow, the greater accessibility of foreign travel, and wide circulation of illustrated art publications, we were brought nearer to the West. [As a result] we saw our own art from a different point of view. Our requirements for the art of painting became much more exacting. We realized that the artistic standard of our painting was low. [This was written in 1902].

Consequently the tendency was to allow the purely pictorial element to dominate the content of an artistic creation, as was also the case in music, where it was required that in a composition the pure tonal mode should dominate the descriptive side. But the World of Art was not satisfied with this. As in literature, the matter was not confined solely to preoccupation with form, and attacks were directed not just at the "poor brush work" of the Itinerants, but more particularly at their subject-matter, which reflected a positivist conception of the world. Therefore the new school undertook the task of replacing this content with an opposite one. As the Itinerants were concerned with the vital issues of the day, it became the aim of the new trend to shun these topics.

Actually its founders—A. Benois (b. 1870), Somov (b. 1869), and Lanceray (b. 1875)—did not escape very far from the present. They focused their study on the St. Petersburg art of the Empire period, and through it they passed to the artistic restoration of its original source, eighteenth-century French art. From Tsarskoe Selo to Versailles, from the Russian *petit-maîtres* to the French marquis, such was the circle of their themes. Igor Grabar (b. 1871), another member of the group, departed further from modernity in an exhaustive study of the origins of Russia's national art. Of course the World of Art acquainted the public also with modern Western masters, chiefly through foreign articles translated into Russian, but it omitted the very newest trends, of which we shall speak later in connection with the still younger generation. It was this comparative conservatism of the founders of the World of Art that permitted some artists of different trends to join the group. Even Repin for a while was a member, although he soon broke this connection as a result of a sharp dispute concerning the merits of some well-known painters and of the Academy, of which he was the dean.

If the members of the World of Art had no clear idea of the future before them, they were determined at least to break away from the past. But the past was linked to the present by many threads which, running parallel to what they had undertaken, and without actually breaking with the Russian tradition of artistic realism, introduced into it new motifs that had remained alien to the Itinerants. The general tendency of the representatives of the new intermediate trend in painting was the same as that of the "World Artists." It was a longing either to withdraw from reality or to find in it something mysterious and super-sensuous that escaped uninitiated eyes. But these aspirations were directed by them along different lines from those of the founders of the World of Art.

The World of Art itself had already indicated one of these lines: the way back to the past. Apart from the archaeological restoration of the past, as undertaken by Grabar, there was yet the task of its artistic reproduction, which was the more interesting because traditionally these themes were in the exclusive possession of the Academy. In this field there was a predecessor of whom the World

Artists made an exception in their general condemnation of academic historical painting. This predecessor was Schwartz, an amateur artist, whose works had been exhibited during the fifties and who died when still young. "Thanks to him we were able to see past events in their true light without the tawdry brilliance so conspicuous in Bruellow's 'Siege of Pskov.'" But above all it was Surikov's (1848–1916) works that the members of the new school singled out for exceptional praise. They made it clear, however, that what they valued in his "Streltsy" and "Boiarynia Morozova" was not so much the artist's historical conception as the purely pictorial side of his creation. To support this point of view they placed great emphasis on Surikov's own admission that his inspiration for the "Streltsy" came from accidentally noticing the reflection of a burning candle on a white shirt, and for his "Boiarynia Morozova" from seeing a black crow with one outspread wing resting on the snow. Attention was also drawn to broad technique, the "rhythm" in composition, and the "orchestration" of color in his works. But of course it was not these artistic merits alone that made Surikov's paintings true epics equal to those of Repin.

The two other fields in which new tendencies began to develop even before the appearance of the World of Art were those of landscape and portrait painting. Here again the World Artists, so severe in their condemnation of the Itinerants, made an exception of two members of the group, the landscape painters Klodt (1832–1902) and Shishkin (1831–98). Both were acknowledged to be "the forerunners of our marvelous poets of native landscape." Not in the tonality, of course, but the drawing. It was a different matter with Kuindzhi (1840–1910), who had seen the works of the French Impressionists in Paris and had brought thence his bright colors, "the equal of which could not be found in the Russian art of the period." But while praise was awarded Kuindzhi for being "so daringly true to nature," he was blamed for "leaning towards cheap effects, theatrical tricks, and a desire to please the crude taste of the crowd." According to the World Artists, the new era in the history of Russian landscape painting began with Savrasov's picture "The Rooks Have Come" (1871), in which they saw revealed the "divine gift of hearing the mysterious voices of nature." It was Levitan (1861–1900) who possessed this divine gift to the highest degree, and yet even his works were criticized. It was emphasized that the very name of his picture called "A Haven of Rest" suggested the artist's intention of transmitting a mood—and not by means of color at that, for color had no scope in the "peaceful and unassumingly charming Russian landscape."

Levitan had to experience a great inner struggle before he could break away from the past, and this definitely undermined his delicate health. But Constantine Korovin (b. 1861) had a different nature. He foresook the past with no struggle whatsoever and became the "first real Russian Impressionist." After a visit to Paris he at once appropriated all the devices of the impressionist technique, and his pictures became "fountains of color" and "feasts for the eye." The limited size of an easel painting was too small for Korovin's wide sweep of the brush. He was the first of the World Artists to paint scenery, but soon his example was followed by Golovin, Bakst, Benois, Bilibin, and Sudeikin, and thus artistic painting was introduced to the stage. It was due to Diagilev's untiring efforts that Europe came to know this particular type of Russian art.

N. Roerich occupies a special place in the field of landscape painting. An archaeologist by profession, he was not content with present day or historical subjects, but sought his themes in prehistoric legends. In this sphere he could freely unfold his particular talent of a colorist. A disregard of line for the sake of color, and the painting of large surfaces with solid color were the two impressionist methods broadly applied by Roerich. Moreover, in his pictures he always emphasized the element of mystery, and in the course of time it became the dominating trait. A prolific artist, Roerich was equally well known for his easel painting and his stylized stage settings. Stylization, which had made some progress in the works of other members of the group, with Roerich became a fundamental principle of art. Human beings assumed the likeness of inanimate objects, and clouds and stones that of people. In his choice of themes he passed from the weird cliffs and lakes of Finland, painted in a color scheme suggesting either the creation or the end of the world, to the mysteries of the cities of India, and finally to the divine secrets of the Himalayas and Tibet. Exoticism led Roerich away from Russia to American skyscrapers, where his canvases found permanent shelter. This fact shows once again how cosmopolitan was that particular type of Russian art.

When approaching the new achievements in Russian portrait painting it is well to remember that realism had always prevailed in this field. The romantic classicist Bruellow, though artificial in his historical and allegorical compositions, was a perfect realist in portrait painting, and created works which outlived his school. To some extent the same is true of Gay (1831–94), Kramskoy (1837–87), Repin, and a number of other artists. The period of protest against the Itinerants also produced a remarkable portrait painter, Valentine Serov (1865–1911), a pupil of Repin, whose earlier pictures had been shown at the Itinerant Exhibitions. By introducing into his art some of the World Artists' tendencies, he gained the recognition of the new school and became associated with it. At the same time Serov remained true to realism even when trying to "spiritualize" it by other than purely pictorial means. To understand the psychology of his model was one of Serov's chief preoccupations, resulting in "not only wonderful pieces of painting, but also very clever, very subtle, and very convincing characterizations" (Benois). Serov's achievements, as is known, cost him great and painstaking efforts. Not satisfied with the mastery of color, he assiduously sought the "line," the true stroke that would at once supply the characteristic trait. But in all these pursuits he never verged on stylization and retained his realism. This type of realism necessitated the introduction of a new term—"neo-realism."

The new spiritual currents which had difficulty in breaking through the inherent realism of landscape and portrait painting sought for themselves, and found, a wider sphere in the fairy world of Russian folklore and in religious painting, where stylization and color could be developed to any desired extent. But even in this field the movement began rather unassumingly, and at first avoided overstepping too pointedly the confines of realism. Its initiator, Victor Vasnetsov (b. 1848), belonged to the generation of the Itinerants and was never fully recognized by the younger artists. His "Alenushka," "The Knights at the Crossroad," "Ivan Tsarevich," and "The Three Tsarevnas of the Subterranean Kingdom," all painted during the eighteen-eighties, were efforts to penetrate into the realm of fairy tale and *bylina* (epic folklore), but were judged unsatisfactory by the new school because in them Vasnetsov still adhered too much to realism. They were not "visions" but actual, living people in the midst of real nature, although compared with Polenov's (b. 1844) frankly realistic works they undoubtedly represented an approach to idealism. Vasnetsov's ideas were a novelty in Russia and as such could not fail to arouse intense feeling and argument among both artists and the public. His transition from the subjects of fairy tale to the painting of frescoes at the Cathedral of the Assumption in Kiev (1886) was accompanied by rumors that there would be created something "great and holy, a new revelation." Vasnetsov obviously aspired to the crown of laurels Ivanov had failed to attain. When ten years later the work was finished, those who saw it were amazed at the unusual blending of Byzantine tradition with modern technique. His Madonna, with her enormous eyes and coquettish posture, brought Vasnetsov great popularity. But this time the young artists were right when they refused to acknowledge him as the one to revive national religious art. They compared Vasnetsov's work with the recently rediscovered ancient Russian icon, and the comparison was to his detriment. The young generation showed a preference for their contemporary Nesterov (b. 1862), though in their opinion his collaboration with Vasnetsov on the frescoes of the Cathedral in Kiev had rather corrupted him. Nesterov's icons were considered to be "as sugary and manneristic as Vasnetsov's artificial creations," but he received recognition for "the poetry of his prayerful moods, the gentle ecstasies, the wonderful visions and revelations," harmonizing so perfectly with his landscape. Scenes from monastic life and visions of the ascetics were unfolded by him against the austere background of the Russian North, where many of the Russian saints had lived, and many of the hagiographic legends had originated.

The younger artists, Roerich (b. 1874), Bilibin (b. 1876), and the solitary Vrubel (1856–1910), naturally moved forward more daringly in this sphere of legend and folklore. Vrubel in particular should be singled out for the grandiosity of conceptions, the intense, incessant quest of new forms of beauty, and the acute and morbid feeling that his accomplishments could never equal his aspirations. His mastery of tonality, which attained perfection in his "Pearl" and "The Demon," his attempts at a creative reincarnation of nature, and his near approach to the mood of a true religious artist—all these were but fragments of that to which he aspired. Insanity and death put an end to the struggle with his own ideal, the realization of which proved to be beyond his strength.

In separating the original group of the World Artists from those who came from the outside to follow their banner, we may now ask ourselves what innovations were introduced into the history of art, and into art itself by the enthusiastic founders of this group. This point can be elucidated by a reference to their own declaration, which bears the signature of Serge Diagilev (1872–1929). "It is always easy to *repudiate*," it says, "and with our usual, cherished scepticism we have attained perfection in this matter. But what ought we to *proclaim* instead, how should we discriminate in our choice from the unclassified and chaotic property left to us by our fathers, when nothing but the revaluation of the countless treasures we have inherited would occupy the life time of our generation?" "How can we, who seek only individuality and believe only in ourselves, possibly take for granted the convictions and arguments of our fathers and forefathers?" is Diagilev's next question. The first half of this sentence is somewhat qualified by the following reservation: "We are more broad-minded than anyone has ever been. We admire *everything*, but we see it from our own point of view, and in this and only in this sense do we admire ourselves." At first glance, this suggests a renunciation of originality and acceptance of eclecticism, so abhorred by the new school. Yet eclecticism remained alien to the new group, which possessed, on the contrary, extreme self-assertion, almost verging on obsession. But has this self-assertion any positive content? Again Diagilev says: "We then emerged with new demands, confirming by our very appearance the validity of the general law of historical development. True, we differed somewhat from the established artistic standards, and we took a few timid and innocent steps turning aside from the great highway, and because of this we were called the children of decadence." Is that accusation fair? Yes and no. "We represent another sad epoch," continues Diagilev, "when art, having attained the zenith of its maturity, sheds the last slanting rays of the setting sun over an aging civilization. It is not the new generation that is decadent, but all the three principal trends of art that have replaced one another during the nineteenth century—classicism, romanticism, and realism. As to ourselves, we remain sceptical observers refuting and accepting in an equal manner every effort made prior to our time."

Diagilev is willing to recognize that "children frequently have a truly childish desire to do everything their fathers have not done, and to pride themselves on their excesses." But he professes surprise at "the shortsightedness of the fathers who rise to the bait of the children's provocation. Why . . . do they not understand that every new epoch is always crowded . . . with many extremes, which . . . should be rejected . . . as one does the superfluous shell that covers the true kernel?" Moreover Diagilev insists—and not without foundation—that in the case of the World Artists the "children" were not guilty of real excesses. "It is ridiculous and foolish to judge our epoch by the paintings of Van Gogh and La Rochefoucauld or the literary works of Mallarmé and Lewis. These are ludicrous and unconvincing examples. Epochs should only be judged by the serious elements that express them and not by the few casual celebrities."

These statements deserve further consideration. It should be admitted that the World of Art actually stood apart from those extremes which the "children" of the next generation were to regard as the true norm of art. The World Artists turned to the past—and a far distant one at that—for their models instead of looking for them in the present, and they deserve credit for reviving the memory of that past. Their sole indisputable authority on modern art was Whistler, and among the Impressionists they studied in detail only the works of Degas. While struggling with the national Russian school and trying to show the benefits of a new alliance with the West, they nevertheless treated the question of national element in art most cautiously. If, on the one hand, "nothing could be more ruinous for a creative artist than a studious attempt to *become* national," then, on the other hand, "the very nature of the artist must be national, and it must involuntarily, or even at times against his will, reflect the true national spirit." From this point of view the World Artists condemned the efforts of the conscientious seekers after nationality in art and their superficial use of the

supposedly typical national traits as a fatal mistake. And yet, when
it came to exporting the new Russian art, Diagilev himself did not
hesitate to choose deliberately these very "superficial traits" as the
ones most likely to attract public interest abroad. In fact, it was
this exotic combination of lines, movement, melody, and harmony
that accounted for the tremendous success of the Russian ballet,
operatic music, and scenery in Europe. But did this mean the
creation of a true national style? It would have been a great
achievement, but we dare not attribute it to the World Artists.
Undoubtedly they deserve credit for their efforts to create a Russian style in furniture, ornaments, embroideries, and the like, but
even here the national style was too crowded with elements of the
style moderne and the unassimilated recollections of ancient Russian art, to produce any impression of final achievement.

Thus the World of Art activities definitely left room for the
following generation to discover new ways of artistic progress. In
their attempts the newcomers first repudiated much of all that had
been accepted by the World Artists, and then as a point of departure they chose exactly what Benois and Diagilev had regarded as
"excess" and "shell." The World of Art group had come to modernity by the way of history, and had endeavored throughout to
maintain a certain historical objectivity. The new "children,"
frankly ignorant of history, had no desire to be objective even in
the Diagilev sense of the word.

This discord between the new generation and the World Artists
became apparent rather soon. As early as 1906, we find in *Golden
Fleece,* an article by Benois on the "Artistic Heresies," with a sharp
formulation of the issues over which he differed with the young
artists. "The generation now maturing and which will replace
us," wrote Benois, "is carried away by individualism, and despises
canons, schools, and tradition." In his opinion this individualism
is heresy, because it repudiates all "fellowship." "True art is only
alive in schools where the artists center around a definite dogma."
"An individual ego detached from everything outside of its sphere
can scarcely possess intrinsic value." "But what do the artists do?
They seek their own corners, find pleasure in self-adulation . . .
striving only to be themselves. Such strictly imposed individualism
is absurd and leads a human being to the primitive state. At the

present time, the position created for art," Benois concludes, "is unprecedented. . . . It resembles mostly the epoch of the downfall of ancient Rome, or Byzantinism."

In publishing Benois' article the editors of the periodical found it necessary to state that his point of view differed from theirs. Moreover, on the pages of the same magazine there subsequently appeared serious objections coming from Shervashidze, Milioti, Voloshin, and others.[3] Shervashidze wrote: "The barbaric invasion is a fresh vigor of life. It is beyond our power to restrain it. Life is ever creating new forms, and the new forms of life demand new art. . . . How it will materialize we do not know, but we believe firmly in the inexhaustible power of life." Milioti made a bitter attack on the World of Art, accusing it of a "drawing-room spirit" and the World Artists of having banished from art "all the drama of spiritual emotions and reduced to insignificance the fundamental function of art by their refined aestheticism." "All religious feeling was forgotten," Milioti wrote in another article; "Christ and His Apostles . . . were replaced by cupids and manneristic ladies and gentlemen. . . . The soul degenerated, grew thin, and assumed a form too fragile and ethereal." His decided opinion was that "Russian art faced a fateful question: either to retire into itself, expand the range of refined emotions, and serve as entertainment to a sympathetic but restricted group, or else to broaden and deepen . . . our inner emotions, be unafraid of the imperious demands of objective life, and thus become really indispensable." Voloshin likewise emphasized the social motive, combining it with a formula the full significance of which we shall see later on.

The task of art is not that it should reflect life like a mirror, but that it should transform, uplift, and fashion every moment of existing nature. Art is the justification of life. That is why painting must reach beyond the confines of a framed picture, which is absolutely alien to the interior decoration and architecture of modern dwellings. The creation of objects surrounding man has actually passed into factory hands; artists have lost the opportunity to participate immediately in the re-creation of life.

[3] See *Golden Fleece*, 1906, II, V, VI; 1907, V; 1909, IV.

The art of painting had to advance a long way from the stand taken by the World Artists in order to arrive at this conclusion. In the West a similar evolution had required about half a century for its completion. Russian art had missed the initial stage of this newest development, but subsequently it went through the process at an accelerated pace, skipping over several stages and thus being able to overtake the latest Western achievements in some twenty or twenty-five years. Throughout this period Paris remained the chief source of influence and inspiration.

The new period in the history of modern art in Western Europe had been ushered in by Impressionism, but at first Russian art remained impervious to the influence of that school. There was no need for it to adopt from the Impressionists such features as their protest against academism, their idea of painting nature and life unadorned, or their democratic bohemianism with its preference for subjects taken from country life or scenes observed in city taverns. Even the Impressionist technique, particularly the *pleinairism,* as we know, was not entirely new to Russia. In fact, Russian artists found their own national way to sincerity and simplicity exactly at the time when in Paris a parallel movement led Corot, Courbet, and Millet to Realism, and the disciples of Eduard Manet to Impressionism. Moreover, the Itinerants temporarily interrupted the heretofore continued dependence of Russian art on that of the West. When, at the end of the nineteenth century, the connection was reëstablished, the Russians were facing a completed cycle of Western progress, from which they could take whatever material they chose. But they did not become blind imitators. The Russian artists of the new generation had their own way of protesting against the literary character of the Itinerants' works, as expressed in the predominance of subject over manner in painting, and this drew them closer to Impressionism, in which they also found this very quality advanced by the Impressionists as a peculiarity of the school: *la bonne peinture* expressed in a new manner of using color, often to the detriment of form and drawing. The tendency towards vivid coloring was traditional in Russia, and here the discoveries of the Impressionists fell on fertile ground. The first Russian propagandist of this particular Impressionist achievement was Kuindzhi, who as early as the eighteen-eighties brought the innovation from Paris, and subsequently transmitted the art of color to his pupils, Roerich and Constantine Bogaevsky.

The first real Impressionist of Russia, Constantine Korovin, had also studied in Paris, yet, notwithstanding the Impressionist technique, he remained true to his native Russian originality. In his work of decorating the Russian pavilion at the Paris Exhibition of 1900 the French people saw for the first time the fruits of Russian art's alliance with modern painting. At the same exhibition the Russian colorist Maliavin (b. 1869) absolutely astounded the public with the vast sea of red color in the dashing parade of his "Babas" (Peasant Women). In this connection we must mention another outstanding Russian colorist, Golovin (b. 1863), a pupil of the Itinerants, who collaborated with Korovin both at the exhibition and again in later days, but who acquired his mastery of color only after repeated visits (1905-07) to Italy and Spain.

The final years of the nineteenth century were those during which the outstanding Russian artists came into closer contact with the newest trends of foreign painting. It was significant that the group which raised the banner of cosmopolitanism in art called itself the "World of Art." This world was as though rediscovered in Russia, and not only the youth, but even the mature artists helped themselves from its treasure chest. Naturally they preferred what was most modern, and the enthusiasm of the moment was for the Post-Impressionists—Cézanne, Van Gogh, and Gauguin—while both the founders of Impressionism and the Neo-Impressionists were relegated to the past. This process of intimate acquaintance with the recent trends in Western art was greatly assisted by the Russian artists' frequent visits abroad and, even on a wider scale, by exhibitions, which shortly acquired a cosmopolitan character. In 1898 Diagilev began his artistic career by holding an exhibition of Russian art, in 1899 he organized an international one, which in 1900 was followed by the first of the World of Art, while the works of Russian artists appeared also that same year at the Paris Exhibition. Under Diagilev's management the Exhibition of Russian Art was held in 1906 at the Paris Autumn Salon, and almost simultaneously the famous seasons of Ballet Russe were inaugurated.

But what was the result of this closer union between Russian art and Western Europe? The foreigners saw instantly that the Russians were not slavishly imitating their art, but were showing something original and unknown to them, which was accepted as being exotic—even barbaric, perhaps—but nevertheless unusual and worthy of recognition.

In order to understand what was peculiarly Russian in this art we must pause at the transient figure of Borisov-Musatov (1870–1905), a gifted artist who died prematurely.

Musatov endowed French technique with his sensitive and tender Russian soul, and to him more than to anybody else we can apply P. Muratov's remark that in spite of all the influx of Western influences, new Russian art succeeded in preserving its intimate and profound character, its religious longing, and its pure lyricism. One must point out, however, that this Russian painter's mood was neither accidental nor unusual, but coincided with that period in the development of contemporary art in Western Europe which ordinarily is referred to as Expressionism. This "art of inner emotions" found its home not so much in the clear and cold atmosphere of France as in that of the misty and sentimentally romantic North. While it would be useless to seek the direct sources of influence upon Musatov in France, it is rather easy to find parallels for his art in northern Europe. In France the term Expressionism signified merely an antithesis to Impressionism, whereas in Germany it developed into *Weltanschauung,* and to be an Expressionist was to portray the soul (*Seeie malen*). The only Post-Impressionist in France who aspired to portray the soul was Van Gogh, a Dutchman. Another artist whose mood was like Musatov's was Munch, a Norwegian with a dreamy northern soul and a tendency towards melancholy, who brought the French Expressionist technique from Paris to Germany. Although in some respects Musatov resembled these Western artists, he was typically Russian in replacing urbanism with a poetical representation of a country manor. His favorite theme was young women, pale and delicate, in old-fashioned and rather provincial costumes, passing like shadows in the evening twilight against the background of autumnal foliage.

Musatov was neither a chance phenomenon in the history of

Russian painting nor an exception. A group of artists, among whom were some of his intimate friends, first exhibited their Expressionist works with the World of Art and then, in 1907, at their own exhibition called "The Blue Rose," which, as S. Makovsky promptly pointed out, was a definite protest against the tendency of the World Artists.

It is important to note that some members of "The Blue Rose" already went beyond Expressionism. Yet, generally speaking, various trends of contemporary Western art were adopted in Russia with such haste that the evolution of Russian painting during that period was not able to follow any strict order of logical consecutiveness. Before the recently introduced and still largely unfamiliar Expressionism had time to assert itself, new and more radical tendencies began to clamor for recognition. At that stage, as Makovsky expressed it, "the last link between painting and the material side of the world which it pretended to picture was definitely lost." The two outstanding representatives of the trend in question—M. Larionov and Natalie Goncharova—were born in the same year (1881). They studied together at the School of Painting, Sculpture, and Architecture in Moscow, and subsequently continued to work in close association. They both experienced the same foreign influences, and both sought inspiration at the popular Russian sources of primitivism. The art critics have established the following three periods in the succession of various foreign influences in the works of both Larionov and Goncharova:

> 1900–1905, Impressionism and Secessionism;
> 1906–1911, Cubism and Primitivism;
> from 1912, Futurism and Radialism.

The chronology of this scheme is significant. We see from it that the Russian innovators had overtaken the West at the second stage, and even attempted to outdistance it at the third, illustrating thereby the general law of accelerated development characteristic of Russian art of the period. The influence of Impressionism was amply recorded in a series of Larionov's works, painted from 1903 to 1905, after the latest manner of Claude Monet and representing "Rose Bushes" and "Corners of a Barn" under various effects of light at different hours of the day and night.

As indicated above, the critics found in the art of Larionov and

Goncharova, besides Impressionism, another foreign influence—Secessionism. The reference here is to the German "Secession," particularly the Munich group, which arose in 1912 under the name of "The Blue Horseman" (*Der Blaue Reiter*) : Franz Marc, Basil Kandinsky, and others. Both Larionov and Goncharova were invited to participate in "The Blue Horseman" exhibition, where they were to meet with the most extreme examples of the breach between art and nature. But, as we shall see, they were already fully prepared for that. The tempo in the shift of art's latest ideas had by that time become positively feverish, and the Moscow artists, followed by their St. Petersburg colleagues, did everything in their power not to lag behind Europe.

In December 1910 and January 1911 Larionov organized an exhibition in Moscow under the name of "The Knave of Diamonds." At that time Larionov and Gorcharova were considering themselves Cubists, a reasonable claim because of their simplified drawing. A series of exhibitions followed and all were filled with the works of these prolific artists.

It was natural that so much ado and energy should lead to imitation, the more so because the primitive manner, the simplified drawing, and particularly the geometric structures detached from any subject, were easy to copy and did not require special training. The "Union of Youth," with David Burliuk as its most prominent member, was formed at that time in St. Petersburg. During the winter seasons of 1911–13 a vociferous propaganda of Futurism was started, and both in St. Petersburg and Moscow there were numerous and highly animated debates on modern art. Confusion increased when the original Moscow innovators decided to dissociate themselves from many of their followers and imitators, whom they accused of having vulgarized their ideas beyond recognition. This they did in a rather pretentious declaration issued by Larionov and Goncharova, jointly with nine other artists, in an introduction to the catalogue of their exhibition of 1912–13. Besides criticizing all other schools, including the Cubist and Futurist, the declaration attempted also to formulate the positive aims of the group. "Art for life or rather life for art. . . . Genius pervades the style of our time—our trousers, coats, shoes, tramcars, automobiles, airplanes, railroads, gigantic steamers

—so fascinating—such a great epoch, the like of which has never existed in the history of the world." Here the authors of the declaration formally joined the ranks of urbanists and expressed their enthusiasm for the machine age. But further they announced two other principles, having no connection with the first and even antagonistic to it: "Long live the beautiful Orient! We join modern Oriental artists for concerted work," and "Long live nationality! We walk hand in hand with the house painters."

This dualism, in fact, was typical throughout the art of Larionov and Goncharova. It was at one and the same time cosmopolitan and national and it found its inspiration both in the latest Western ideas and in the Eastern primitives.

We shall return presently to the national and Oriental traits of their art, but first we must follow to the end the line of their Western adoptions. We know that Larionov had scarcely had time to become a Cubist when in the West Cubism developed into Futurism. Larionov, however, was not satisfied with a mere imitation of foreign artists, and so he unfolded his own theory, which he called "Radialism." In opposition to the Impressionist method of painting in planes, Cubism wanted to conquer space by organizing it into geometric structures. Futurism added to that the organization of movement in space, and as this touched upon the problem of time in space it led the mind to the regions bordering on science and metaphysics. Radialism followed along these lines. "Science tells us," Larionov reasoned, "that we see all objects through the medium of rays that emanate from them. Therefore, strictly speaking, we do not actually see the object as such, but only the sum of rays which coming from the source of light are reflected by the object and enter into the field of our vision." Consequently, painting must represent not the visible objects but "certain forms selected by the artist's own will and generated by the intersection in space of the reflected rays of various objects." In works painted according to this theory the uninitiated spectator sees nothing but a chaos of intersected lines, with clusters of "rays" issuing in disorder from some points of intersection.

This part of Larionov's and Goncharova's art could not fail to provoke the liveliest controversies, and if it survived these polemics it was due to its other aspect. The fact is that in trying to find patterns for their simplified painting, these artists bethought themselves of the original source of the Russian primitive—popular art. Did not Gauguin show enthusiasm for the art of Negroes and Aztecs, and did not the Russian adversaries of the Itinerants look for primitives in ancient icon painting? Then why not resort to the more immediately accessible forms of popular art, such as Russian lace, toys, snuffboxes, trays, or even the commercial signs made by provincial sign painters? That was the meaning of the formula "nationality and the Orient." The new art's passion for these sources was, of course, an exaggerated one; but undeniably it led the two artists to a great variety of new motifs, particularly of the ornamental type, and enabled them to develop their talents as colorists.

It was exactly this side of Russian art that had already brought it in touch with the West on a more or less equal footing. Here the Russian art abandoned the cosmopolitanism of mere imitators of the newest French and German trends for a genuine folk element. Although in itself this is not sufficient for an art to become truly national, yet it was actually this quality of the new Russian art that produced the greatest impression abroad. This brings us to the export of Russian art, which is associated with the world-famous Ballet Russe and the name of its chief organizer, Serge Diagilev.

When Diagilev started his enterprise all its essential elements were in readiness. In his earlier career he had gradually become the master of the three branches of art, which he later amalgamated in the Ballet Russe. He began by organizing exhibitions of the World Artists, then, being also something of a musician, he formed connections with the new generation of Russian composers, and finally, because he had served in the management of the Imperial Theatres, he had acquired familiarity with the classical ballet. In 1906 Diagilev brought Russian paintings to Paris; in 1907 he acquainted the Parisians with Russian music (Historical Concerts), and in 1909 he inaugurated the Ballet Russe, which for twenty years, until his death in 1929, continued to unfold its fairy-like pageant, if not always from success to success, at least from one sensation to another. With the genius of a born impresario, Diagilev realized that the ballet was the best form of art to make his enterprise popular among foreigners, but his greatest achievement was the skill with which he combined the three branches of art— Russian scenery painting, Russian choreography, and Russian music—into a single masterpiece, possessing such peculiar freshness, vividness, and vigor.

The outstanding trait of the Ballet Russe, which enabled it to fascinate foreigners and to win their immediate recognition, was its exoticism. Here was something never seen before, something that carried the audience away from everyday surroundings into the world of fairy tales. This peculiar quality of the new Russian art was, indeed, due to its intimate connection with the national folklore, a circumstance attributable not only to a passing fashion, but to the general conditions of Russia's cultural development, which accounted for the tenacity and vitality of the popular element in art. Thus Tugendhold was perfectly right when, in replying to Marcel Prévost, who attempted to prove that the ballet could attain perfection only under a monarchy, he argued that although such was, undoubtedly, the historical origin of the ballet in Russia, its modern achievements had nothing in common with it.[4] They were based chiefly on folk dances and the "dancing tradition still flourishing among the Russian people." Equally indisputable is the fact that folk song and rhythm have played an important part in modern Russian music, and that the vivid, clear colors of popular art have inspired the scenery and the costumes created by Russian colorists. One can add to this the element of iconographic archaism, which is very evident in Bilibin's conventionalized drawing, and the Oriental element which permeates all modern Russian dances, music, scenery, and costumes. Tugendhold also mentioned two other important features—the chorus-like discipline in the movements of both the solo dancers and the supernumeraries, and the "truth in movement" corresponding to "truth in sound," which created the impression of spontaneity and sincerity. Finally, it must be pointed out that for the majority of Diagilev's productions the subjects were taken either from Russian folklore or from Oriental tales, two sources particularly conducive to the development of all the above-mentioned traits.

Through the medium of this complex and well-integrated art,

4 See his article in *Apollo*, 1910, X.

foreigners were brought in touch with a virtually unfamiliar culture, shown to them in its most peculiar aspects and with an emphasis upon its primitive side. Because of this, the impression produced was unusually strong and at the same time disturbing. The Ballet Russe was unanimously acclaimed at first, but voices were raised in protest when it became a regular item of the Paris winter season. Besides the nationalists' discontent with the predominance of Russians, there was also the "incompatibility of soul." This feeling became particularly strong each time that Diagilev tried to introduce into his repertory some productions adapted from Western subjects or the music of Chopin, Schubert, and Debussy. In 1912 Lalo wrote in connection with the production of *L'Après-midi d'un faune:* "The Russians have provided us with many beautiful pictures and helpful lessons, but they are contributing to the deterioration of our taste with their passion for gorgeous and brilliant pageants, whose only aim is to delight the eye. Actually, it is barbarism disguised as refined art. *La marque des barbares est sur eux."* The French people were also somewhat disconcerted by the lavish settings of the Ballet: the bright, vivid coloring of the Russian palette, the subtle voluptuousness of Bakst's costumes, Sudeikin's saturnalia of color, Bilibin's conventionalized drawing, Goncharova's primitives, and Larionov's geometric structures—all containing a vast amount of orientalism and primitivism. These fountains of color and chromatic feasts were in too great a contrast with the faded subdued shades of contemporary fashion and the intentionally modest theatrical productions which in those days avoided strong scenic effects and completely lacked harmony in the scenery, costumes, and music.

Here we must stress the fact that it was the Russian part of the Diagilev Ballet, which during the first five years was its outstanding feature, that received unreserved recognition abroad. During those early years the Ballet relied almost entirely on the accumulated artistic resources of the Imperial Theatres, and the collaboration of the World Artists. But this initial success soon came to an end. The repeated production of the old ballets no longer aroused the former enthusiasm. It was necessary to progress with the times, which meant making the Ballet more European and introducing upon the stage artistic novelties from Montmartre and Montparnasse, resulting in the stormy controversy that arose in Parisian artistic circles. As Diagilev always welcomed new ideas, even at the risk of failure, he abandoned his earlier exoticism, which had been unquestioningly accepted by foreigners as the national Russian style, and fearlessly followed the latest Parisian vogue, winning thereby the approval of a few connoisseurs and the general resentment of the public. Gradually Benois and Bakst were replaced by Goncharova and Larionov; Borodin and Rimsky-Korsakov by Stravinsky and Prokofiev; Fokin, Nizhinsky, and the two ballerinas of the Imperial Ballet, Anna Pavlova and Karsavina, by Miasin, Nizhinskaia, and Lifar, all three trained by Diagilev. Simultaneously the leaders of modern European art were brought to the forefront: Debussy, Ravel, Florent Schmitt, and Erik Satie replaced Chopin and Schumann, while Picasso, Matisse, Derain, Gris, Marie Laurencin, and Utrillo took the places of the Russian scenery painters. Only the staff of the Ballet could not be replaced. This actual coöperation of foreign and Russian artists contributed largely to the further development of Russian art. It must be added, however, that the second and longest period of the Ballet Russe, which began in 1914 with the production of Picasso and Satie's "Parade," belongs mostly to post-war days, when Russia was already cut off from the rest of the world.

What was the foreigners' impression of the Ballet Russe at this second period? The spontaneous recognition of an alien and exotic art was now replaced with a struggle against radical tendencies in Western art itself. In the heat of this struggle Russian artists were looked upon with increasing suspicion as the originators of barbarism in modern art, and even those critics who at first had been fascinated by Russian exoticism now began to feel restive and annoyed. We have a characteristic expression of this attitude in Arsène Alexandre's introduction to the catalogue of the "World of Art" exhibition of 1921.

We thought [he wrote] that after the exhibition of 1906 we understood Russian art. But now, in 1921 . . . it would be unwise to say, 'I understand.' . . . The newest tendencies . . . either abandon themselves in stormy transports, the rhythm of which escapes us, or else they combine inexorable realism with the stolid, elaborate detail work of the primitives. Neither their tradition nor their innovation is the same as ours. Thus, in spite of the fascination their works still exercise upon us, we cannot agree entirely with them in understanding and emotions. Is it possible to transplant to our brain the mentality of another race? . . . The influence of Russian paintings would definitely destroy what little we have preserved of our national genius. That is why I rejoice over these unexpected revelations and at the same time am on the alert against them.

With Diagilev's death in 1929 a note of reconciliation was introduced into this attitude; but it was a reconciliation with something that was forever ended and would never again be repeated. This fact was emphasized in most of the articles published in the commemorative issue of the *Revue Musicale.* *"La superbe folie, le bonheur de l'étrangeté, peut-être faut-il que la beauté meurt,"* wrote Countess de Noailles, the poetess. *"La magie charmante est finie,"* echoed E. Henriot, while Maurice Brillant spoke of a "bygone power," and "an epoch entirely finished and now seeming to us distant. . . ."

These remarks, alluding to the end of the epoch of Ballet Russe, will serve us as a transition from the history to the present state of Russian art. The accelerated rhythm in which the latest trends followed each other and their extreme radicalism were confusing not only to the foreigners but to the Russians as well. We know that in Russia this succession of trends did not possess even that regularity which to some extent it still preserved in the West. In trying to overtake the Western development, Russian art passed far more quickly through these changes and in the process added to them its own eccentricities. As a result in Russia the new ideas had no time in which to take root, and exhausted themselves much sooner than they did in the West. The ultimate outcome was, nevertheless, identical in both cases. In Russia, as in the West, the circle was completed by a return to old artistic traditions and methods. The artists became more independent of the latest fashion and began to express in art their own individuality.

Contrary to the expectations of those who tenaciously predicted a revival of religious painting, attempts in this particular type of art were confined to stylization and intentional archaism. Sometimes, as in the works of Stelletsky, it was nothing but a rather mechanical copying of ancient patterns. The intimate landscape stood on firmer ground, for it was able to combine realism with expression of individual moods, as for example in Kustodiev's village inns and secluded provincial lanes, or in Lakhovsky's picturesque corners of St. Petersburg, Pskov, and other Russian cities. But the trend which could be more easily understood by the foreigners was the return to painstaking execution of details, in the manner of Van Eyck, as seen in the works of A. Iakovlev and Shukhaev. Iakovlev, a prolific artist, presented to the European public many series of realistic pictures of his travels in the Far East and through Central Africa, and of everyday life in France. The realism in these paintings reminds one more of the old Russian Itinerants than it does of Gauguin's exoticism.

A separate place in contemporary Russian art belongs to the artists who have tried to combine realism with the most daring innovation. Boris Grigoriev's (b. 1886) works are a good example of this complex style of painting. Russian life of the moment (the early years of the revolution) supplied this artist with ample material, for it ignored in every possible way all outward conventionalities and presented subjects which would have aroused Van Gogh's envy. Anything that deviated from the normal became the rule, and in the quest to satisfy elementary needs the brute in man came to the fore. A dull bestiality was reflected even in the facial expression of the people. Thus reality approached stylization and caricature, and from it Grigoriev chose the types for his "Russia" and the landscapes of untilled land covered with the yellow ochre of clay and loess. From his awful, inexorably realistic canvases domestic animals look at the spectator with the huge, conscious eyes of man, while human beings are humbled to the level of animals.

Mark Shagal (b. 1887), a contemporary of Grigoriev, is a similar phenomenon. Both artists brought with them to Paris their individual impressions of lonely places in Russia. Shagal's recollections of Vitebsk, his native place, were as vivid as those Grigoriev had of his Russian village. In Paris they both went through the inevitable school of Cubism and conscientiously absorbed its teachings. Then gradually they were emancipated from its dead dullness, and relying on the all-too-vivid impressions of their earlier years, Grigoriev began crowding his canvases with scenes from workaday life of the Russian masses, and Shagal with those of the Jewish Ghetto. But Shagal exceeded Grigoriev in his disregard of all natural laws. In his pictures human beings fly, stand on their heads, sometimes heads are detached from the bodies, attitudes are contrary to all laws of equilibrium, houses are deformed and bent like living beings, men are larger than buildings, and perspective is completely ignored. Without trying to compare the creative power of these two artists, we have apposed them only to show the traits they have in common as being characteristic of this particular phase in the development of Russian art. It was the time when every radical trend soon found itself in an impasse and was repudiated; the time of new pursuits, when talent, liberated from binding doctrines, sought an individual expression in art. In following this course the two artists in question have introduced significant modifications in their earlier style; their latest works show a gradual transition from the heaven (or hell) they had created to solid ground, which no mortal is ashamed to tread.

In describing all these modern trends, we have reached a sphere which lies beyond the revolutionary upheaval that had separated Russia from the emigration. A free and unhampered development of various trends, of course, has been possible only in the emigration. But we know that cultural life has not been at a standstill in Soviet Russia. Therefore we must see now what has taken place in the field of art under the rule of the Bolsheviks.

IV

ART IN SOVIET RUSSIA

THE fate of the figurative arts under the Soviet régime was in many respects similar to that of literature.[1] At first in both fields there was a sharp break between the old and the new. Simultaneously with the obliteration of the past many ultra-radical trends, the very latest fashions in art, appeared in the fore-front. These groups, as those in literature, claimed to represent exclusively a specific revolutionary tendency, and therefore re-garded themselves as being close to the new government and entitled to share in the profits. In both instances these claims were soon found to be largely imaginary. Under the NEP some rem-nants of the old pre-revolutionary trends emerged from conceal-ment, while the relative freedom of the period permitted new sprouts to appear; some combination of the old and the new was attempted, and compromises between them were formulated. Finally, in later years when the government had mastered the situation in both fields, it imposed upon them a centralized control with crushing tendencies which threatened to render all these new shoots barren and to replace the spontaneous inspiration with the formal stamp of "social command." Yet it seems that quite recently there began a new period of reaction against the dead uniformity and submission to government orders.

We will begin with the exodus of the old trends. Their most eminent representatives, such outstanding artists as Maliavin, Korovin, Bilibin, Sudeikin, Sorin, Lakhovsky, Iakovlev, Shukhaev, Grigoriev, Somov, A. Benois, Goncharova, Dobuzhinsky, and Larionov all emigrated to foreign countries; Roerich withdrew

[1] See Part II, chs. 4 and 5.—ED.

to exotic regions, while Repin established himself in Finland. Others who remained in Russia were silent, and in this enforced silence the triumphant cry of the Futurists resounded with great strength and arrogance. The new Bolshevik ideology stimulated the further development of many artistic "isms," which had originated before the revolution. "Collective man" became the slogan for both the Soviet state and Soviet culture. In order not to impede the development of a collective type of "new man," the inner and distinctive private life of an individual had to be set aside. Lenin himself proclaimed that after the destruction of the bureaucratic machine of the modern state "all citizens were to become employees and workers in a state syndicate," and "all should perform the self same work . ... carry out their tasks properly and receive equal remuneration." In echoing Lenin, Bukharin approached the human society as a beehive, where everything was based on a purely social point of view, admitting no trace of spiritual life. In accord with these views the historian Pokrovsky stated that "in an individual the Marxists did not see the creator of history, but only an apparatus by means of which history operates," and that "in the future these apparatuses, probably, will be produced artificially just as electrical accumulators are built at the present time." This theme of a Bolshevik robot was seized upon by both painters and poets. Demian Bedny sang of a marching crowd as of "millions of legs in one body" that has but "one step, one heart, and one will." The powerful people "under whose feet the pavement shakes and who will make the whole universe tremble," became the ideal of the new art. At the word of command this giant must repeat automatically the "rationalized" motions of the workman operating a machine, and the millions of concerted movements of hands, feet, and throats will result in an immense single whole. The transformation of a workman into one of the constituent parts of a machine is well illustrated in Krinsky's drawings, where figures are reduced to a few schematic tetragons, their movements are rectilinear and "rational," and in composition men are fused with parts of the machine. It is characteristic that the Bolsheviks found their ideal of "machinism" in Americanism, and from this point of view Maiakovsky sang of Chicago as "the electro-dynamo-mechanical city, built on a screw and rotating every hour around itself," while Gastev in his appeal for Americanization wrote: "We shall seize upon the storm of the revolution, put into it the pulse of American life, and produce a work that will be as accurate as a chronometer. . . ."

The art of collective man had to be monumental. "Streets are our brushes, squares our palettes," Maiakovsky exclaimed vociferously. At first, this command that everything should be monumental found expression only in enlarging the regular forms to huge dimensions. Immense statues representing the heroes of the revolution—Marx, Engels, Radishchev, Herzen, Chernyshevsky, Stenka Razin, and Bauman [2]—were erected. But, as the work had to be finished rapidly, the statues were made in clay and plaster, and therefore soon nothing remained of these artistic creations. As to the cubist statue of Bakunin,[3] it so offended the workmen that it had to be destroyed. Other methods such as a lavish use of paint, for example, were employed in order to attain this unprecedented effect of grandeur. To celebrate the communist festival at which the collective man shook the pavement with thousands of feet, all the lawns, flower beds, and trees in front of the Grand Theatre at Moscow, were painted with red and purple paint. The crowd gazed with amazement at the sea of paint, which in geometrically intersected planes covered the streets, squares, buildings, and street cars. Thus, abandoning the limited canvases of salons and war-time exhibitions, the dubious art of the Cubists, Futurists, and Suprematists came hopefully out into the open. Carried to the extreme, it now was legalized by the October Revolution [4] that had given it an ideological foundation. The extent of this professional self-assertion was evident in the thousands and thousands of yards of painted linen which covered entire buildings during the celebration of the first Soviet anniversary. Tugendhold interpreted this as an effort at the "blasting and undermining of

[2] Radishchev, Russian liberal of the late eighteenth century, author of the first abolitionist tract in Russian literature. Herzen and Chernyshevsky, early Russian socialists of the mid-nineteenth century. Stenka Razin, leader of a peasant rebellion in the seventeenth century. Bauman, a revolutionary, killed during the civil strife in Moscow in October 1905.—ED.

[3] Bakunin, the famous revolutionary of the mid-nineteenth century, founder of modern anarchism.—ED.

[4] I. e., the revolution that overthrew the Provisional Government and established the Soviet régime.—ED.

old slavish sentiments," covering up the sanctuaries, palaces, and monuments, and effacing their familiar forms. "That was the destructive work exacted by the psychology of the moment"—the psychology of the leaders, of course, for the workmen and peasant masses, according to Shchekotov, "regarded this orgy of color and line with disappointing bewilderment." In fact, Tugendhold himself admitted later that in ten years even those who had inspired this bacchanal regained their senses and ability to distinguish the "true sparks of creative genius from fireworks, ideology from phraseology, and revolutionary projects from irresponsible scheming."

After this chaotic period of Futurist predominance, revolutionary art was called upon to serve the Proletcult,[5] and it was placed under the centralized control of the artistic section of the Department of Figurative Arts (IZO), where systematic regulation replaced the former "liberal anarchy and battle of interests." A state fund and an All-Russian Purchasing Commission were instituted to replace the private Maecenases. The "Augean stables" in the Academy of Arts, that citadel of artistic bureaucracy, were cleaned and transformed into free state workrooms. Their work was given an industrial character tending towards the art of objects and towards factories, mills, commercial schools, and workshops. The new slogan was, "Produce objects, as a cobbler does shoes." The artist was to be but a highly qualified manufacturer, and art was transferred from the streets and squares to the laboratory.

But how was all this expressed on canvas? "Engineerism," that is, the cult of "machinism" and Americanism, was introduced into painting, while "constructivist" and "non-topical" art increased in power. From the studio of Lebedev and Lapshin there emerged numerous "suprematistic" and "cubo-futuristic" works, allegedly destined for the masses, but in fact quite beyond their comprehension. Tugendhold remarked that the attempt to introduce geometrical art into the workmen's clubs provoked a "crisis in club life and a decline in club attendance," in other words, it simply drove the people away.

With the introduction of the NEP the Purchasing Commission

---

[5] Abbreviation for "proletarian culture." See Part II, ch. 4.—Ed.

was abolished, and freedom of supply and demand was proclaimed in its stead. The change naturally displeased the artists whom the Commission had patronized, but the old trends, which up to that time had remained inactive, profited by the new freedom and, like the Fellow Travelers in literature, these artists came forward once more. In the Spring of 1922 the Itinerants held their forty-eighth exhibition, which was followed by that of the Moscow Cézannists, all former members of the "Knave of Diamonds" group. Under the new conditions even the revolutionary artists returned to painting definite subjects. Before long another group was formed that chose "heroic realism" for its battle cry. Being patronized by the trade unions, this group was first allowed to hold a permanent exhibition of paintings on labor subjects, and then, in 1923, on the fifth anniversary of the Red Army, its works were shown at the War Museum and also at the Museum of Revolution, which had been opened during that same year. There was also a revival of portrait painting, and portraits of Lenin and of private individuals were exhibited. This concession to public demand resulted in a stream of people rushing at once to the exhibitions.

The "left" artists, however, soon proved unable to satisfy the demand. Their realism was of an inferior quality. Being trained to produce revolutionary posters, these painters now showed in their other works a notable lack of technical skill. Another accusation brought against the new group was that in its realism it was precisely the heroic that was not to be found. According to the critics, revolutionary passion and dynamic composition, the two most essential elements of the revolutionary art, were lacking in their works. Moreover, heroics were reduced to the level of a simple chronicle, a dry account of events. It was the same accusation that was brought against the Fellow Travelers in literature.

But in depicting everyday life the new group was as successful as were the writers of the same period. Perelman has pointed out that its members were to be seen in the factory, in barracks, at a Congress of the Comintern, or at a Soviet Convention. Yet, in the competent opinion of Tugendhold, it was "more the work of an artistic reporter than genuine art." In these paintings "work was represented as toil, as the grievous lot of the working classes, and not as the conscious labor of the proletarian." Besides, "the dark, drab colors, the lifeless, flabby forms are nothing but legacies of the old Populist point of view which approached labor and life of the people as mere objects of pity." With a few exceptions, the critic could not find a single cheerful, active, or vigorous note. Thus, notwithstanding the "social command," no revolutionary painting was produced by the group of "Heroic Realism."

Another group which was organized at that time (1921) under the name of "Being" consisted of the former members of the "Knave of Diamonds" who were joined by some younger artists. The psychology of these artists seemed untouched by the revolution. In fact, they passed from tormenting psychoanalysis and preoccupation with metaphysical depths to the sheer joy of living. They delighted in nature and color, were effervescing with youth and good health, and not particular as to what was to be painted: a tree, a peasant, a Communist youth, a landscape, or a nude. The whole universe was looked upon as an unbroken still-life, as the pretext for an orgy of rich color and sweeping brush strokes, to the detriment of form. Although in 1925 the "Being" merged with the group of "Heroic Realism," it retained its individual character. The sun, verdure, and atmosphere, the exuberance, freshness, and joy of living of the one contrasted vividly with the gray tones of the other. The public demanded paintings representing ordinary people, their life and daily surroundings, and the artists of the "Being," like the members of other groups, began to produce genre.

As in literature, the struggle between the "left" and "right" trends in art led to an attempt at compromise. There was little of the revolutionary in this compromise, nor did it as yet comply with the command for socialist construction. At this period the most important development in Soviet painting was the gradual drawing together of various trends and their move towards a common ground—an attempt to reproduce in art contemporary life. But this process of sovietization, or renunciation of the "inner sabotage" of early days, here as in literature, was not a capitulation either to the Communist dogma or to the political dictatorship of the Bolsheviks. To use Tugendhold's expression, the "straightening of the artistic front was carried out along the lines of a steady advance towards realism, as the only general and firm base of art."

Had the course of events in Soviet Russia been less turbulent, it is quite likely that this process of a mutual adaptation of old traditions and new ideological demands would have continued in that direction. But in 1928 a crisis occurred in Soviet life which inevitably affected art. In the *Almanac of Literature and Art* for 1929 it was admitted that the preceding year had been "the breaking point in the development of the arts." We shall take advantage of the *Almanac's* data to analyze the character of this crisis.

It was provoked by new demands upon art formulated in official quarters. In the first place, all the artistic groups had to be more precise in revealing their "class face." With the "tempestuous growth of socialist construction" mere words about artists supporting Communism, about their revolutionary art, etc., were no longer sufficient. It was necessary for art to take an active part in the construction. But notwithstanding lengthy discussions, the Soviet critics could not specify just how this active participation should manifest itself, and so they applied themselves all the more vigorously to exposing the forms in which art should not find expression, and condemning in the process all the previous attempts of the artists to approach the ideal of proletarian art. During the latter part of March 1928 this question was presented for debate at the Communist Academy, and the arguments lasted four evenings without, however, reaching any positive conclusions. Yet it was obligatory for the artists to comply with the repeated commands of those in power, and seek new forms or, at least, new formulas for artistic expression. But once again their efforts brought no positive results.

Then, unexpectedly, the string that had been pulled too far to the left snapped, and the organizations, which had been straining beyond their strength in that direction, were swept far to the right. The Soviet artists, who had failed to satisfy the government's social command, reverted to "abstract formal problems," and their works showed the triumph of the purely pictorial element. In 1928 the Society of Moscow Artists was organized in which the successors of the "Knave of Diamonds" and other trends of the pre-revolutionary bourgeois art once again made their appearance. A collective article in the *Almanac* complained that they "had organized their own society and promptly repudiated revolutionary themes [in art]. They maintained a high level of achievement, and under their influence other artists have reverted to expressing purely individual emotions and limiting themselves to landscape, portrait, and still-life painting." What was especially symptomatic, the public, particularly in the provinces, crowded their numerous exhibitions.

Thus did easel painting answer the prophets who had condemned it to failure and complete destruction. The efforts to find new ways of introducing art to the masses did not as yet progress beyond the painting of murals on the walls of workmen's clubs. But there were other branches of art more adapted to carry out the command that art be instilled in proletarian life. We have seen the new artists begin by demanding that pictures be replaced by "objects." What were then the achievements in the "art of objects" or, to use the old-fashioned term, applied or decorative art? In this branch it was not necessary to feel one's way or to invent artificial solutions, for here established forms already existed, and it only remained to endow them with new content. House furnishings, utensils, textiles, rugs, and all the extensive field of the *kustarny* industry (domestic handicrafts), seemed to offer opportunity for creating a new proletarian style. Once again we shall avail ourselves of the data published in the article in the *Almanac,* in which negative instructions are, as usual, definite and explicit. "Away with the aesthetic romanticists of the type of William Morris, with their handicraft production and their struggle against the machine! An end must be put to the break existing between art and factory production and to the industry of luxuries for the few. Long live the aesthetics of engineering, the aesthetics of expediency, the new socially expedient workaday forms!" But when recapitulating the actual achievements in this field, the author of the article arrives at most pessimistic conclusions. "Instead of creating new ones they only revived the old, most backward forms of applied art. Instead of designing new furniture, old pieces were collected from private residences in Moscow and from country manors, and were distributed among the new public buildings and institutions. The production of the state furniture industry was based almost entirely upon old patterns. The predominance of very old designs was likewise to be found in the textile industry."

The article supplies also the explanation of this phenomenon: "The consumer responds to old designs, but not to the limited attempts at introducing new ideas, and, after all, mills are worked for the consumer." And the Soviet ornament? "It has many variations on the themes of the state emblem (the sickle and the hammer), of the five-pointed star, and of parts of the machine. But unfortunately it is distinguished by a great lack of imagination and a primitive monotony of treatment." The problem of clothing was no better: "The list of the latest fashions in clothes was exhausted by the Pioneer (Soviet boy scout) costume and the red kerchief of the working women, which are actually not new. Arch-bourgeois dressmakers continue to work, and old copies of fashion magazines are in great demand." The products of domestic craft industry? "They prosper and unquestionably enjoy success abroad."

Thus we have enumerated all the "objects" the production of which was supposed to lead to the creation of a new proletarian style in the future.

The branches of the figurative arts, which were connected with Soviet propaganda, were in their development a far greater success. Aside from the broad field of "art in motion," or the Soviet cinema, this includes polygraphy and the poster. The Bolsheviks are proud, and quite justly, of their achievements in engraving and graphic art, although it should be remembered that the World of Art had initiated this work. In contrast to "picturesque" and "modernistic" Moscow, St. Petersburg was always regarded as being particularly the city of pure graphics. This was the result of studying the Empire style, which in old St. Petersburg and its suburban palaces was so distinctive and in such contrast to the merchant and decadent architecture of Moscow. The works of such pre-revolutionary artists as A. Benois, K. Somov, Dobuzhinsky, and Mme Ostroumova-Lebedeva continued to be reproduced even under the Bolsheviks. But theirs was a poetic representation of a noblemen's culture, or the life of a disappearing class. The Soviet engravers had to forsake the ideals of Versailles and the erotics of the eighteenth-century "marquises," and represent life in a new way. Moreover, they were obliged to simplify the technique of woodcuts, because delicate outlines could not be satisfactorily reproduced on the poor paper available during the early years of Bolshevism. The Moscow school of engravers, under Favorsky's leadership, began its work in this new spirit—the spirit of the art of objects as opposed to aestheticism. In the treatment of revolutionary subjects, graphic art showed more boldness than did painting. It was easier for it to adopt both the necessary "dynamism in treatment" and the "industrial themes," such as steel bridges, radio towers, etc. However, in spite of all this, Tugendhold admitted that "it would be an empty phrase to assert that new Soviet engravings had won their way into the books for the masses." As of old, valuable illustrated editions remained beyond the reach of the mass consumer. "The art of engraving," stated V. Polonsky, "is leading a miserable existence, for it cannot even reach the very restricted circle of consumers." The needs of the masses continued to be satisfied by cheap, third-rate craftsmen, who filled their productions with "imported bourgeois banalities."

We come at last to the favorite offspring of Soviet propaganda —the poster. A product of urbanism and revolution, it was the modern adaptation of the "Bible of the poor" transferred from a parchment manuscript to a street leaflet, and from the leaflet to a fence or wall. There the poster, like the severe and violent explosion of a bomb or sound of a tocsin, was given unlimited and appropriate use during the civil war years of 1918-20. Neither fine drawing nor complicated subjects were required, and the simpler the poster was, the more likely that it would be able to embody in the most understandable and striking form the popular slogans of the day: "Have you enlisted as a volunteer?" "Help the starved!" "Cossack, with whom are you, with them or with us?" "No surrender of Petrograd!" "Soviet Russia—a camp besieged." "All for defense!" "Who is for the Soviets, and who is against the Soviets?" These are examples of the best posters by the greatest poster painter D. Moor (Orlov). V. Deni (Denisov), who ranked second, continued drawing his burlesque types in the style of pre-revolutionary *Satyricon,* contrasting the old trinity—the Tsar, the priest, and the bourgeois—with the new one: a workman, a peasant, and a Red soldier. In the works of these artists the military poster reached its climax. It is of interest to note that in this field, as in literature, everything with an appeal to the people—the poster, the painted walls of the propaganda trains and boats—had perforce to speak and portray in the language and form of artistic realism. In this respect the poster was an exception to the general rule in the "industrial" and "constructivist" style of painting during the War Communism period.

After 1922 the poster, having played its part as "street art," temporarily lost its political significance and was replaced by cinema posters, commercial advertisement posters, etc., but in recent years it has resumed its political and agitational form and was used for the propaganda of "social construction," not so much on the streets as in workmen's clubs and village reading rooms. Indeed, its themes are no longer the same, the colors are duller, the text dominates the picture, and so the poster has become of graphic assistance to lecturers. The favorite themes of these posters are Soviet elections, grain storage, collectivization, industrialization, and war on religion.

Architecture was placed in a more fortunate position under the Soviet régime than was any other branch of art. If modern architecture is, in general, that of an industrial stage in the development of society, in Soviet Russia industrial work has become the central idea of the new state order and its fetish. Granted that the machine serves as a basis for modern industry, in the case of the Communist régime it determines the entire character of life. And if modern architecture is the universal reflection of this combined power of machine production, it is to be expected that in Soviet Russia the cult of the machine will become its most outstanding characteristic and its principal task. We have already pointed out [6] that the style of architecture depends directly on building material, and that in Russia the national style was created by its native wood. The style established in wooden architecture, as we have seen, was later reproduced in stone. But in Russia, as in the history of architecture throughout the world, each time that a style was created by new building materials the lines of the building, which during the earlier period were of structural importance, gradually acquired a merely decorative, aesthetic significance and were freely applied as ornaments. The further a style

[6] See above, ch. 1.—ED.

is developed the more preponderant becomes the decorative element until it finally covers and dominates the structural lines of the building. This process leads to the degeneration of the original style, as for example in the transition from Renaissance to Baroque during the seventeenth and eighteenth centuries. Through the restoration of the classic Empire style at the end of the eighteenth and the beginning of the nineteenth centuries Russia escaped the influence of the decadent Baroque. But this was not a national solution. It was to be expected that with the development of industry and machinery there would be an end to the imitation of old styles and that an entirely new one, of a strictly structural character, would be created. For a long time it was thought that the new architecture would be one of steel, of which the Eiffel Tower was a perfect example. But steel was replaced by steel and concrete, and soon the development of style depended upon these building materials and, of course, upon the industrial and mechanical nature of the problems it was called to solve. This type of architecture rapidly became popular in Europe and especially in the United States of America. But both in Europe and in America the architects resorted to various decorative methods in order to disguise as much as possible the ascetic severity of the structural lines of the modern buildings. In Russia, however, the tendency as usual was to carry modernism to the extreme; any addition of decorative element was rejected and every effort was applied to work out a strictly and consistently structural style of architecture.

We already know that "constructivism" was assigned an important part in other branches of Soviet art, and that attempts to apply this idea where there was no ground for its application led to great exaggeration and resulted in failure. Architecture was, perhaps, the only sphere where "constructivism" was in its place. Yet even here, instead of beginning with specific tasks, they advanced fantastic projects. Among the Soviet architects Tatlin represented the tendency to replace the old bourgeois forms with a "machine" style that would embody all the outstanding features of the modern world with its dynamic character, its rationalism, and its utilitarian attitude. No wood or stone was to be used in these structures; they were to be built entirely of metal, concrete, and glass. Tatlin's plans for the Palace of Labor in Moscow and

for the Monument of the Third International in St. Petersburg
were to serve as examples of this "dynamo-monumental style."
The latter was to be a huge edifice with three stories built in the
shape of a cube, a pyramid, and a cylinder, each in turn to revolve
perpetually—yearly, monthly, and daily. The ground floor was
intended for meetings of legislative institutions and congresses of
the Comintern, the second for executive agencies, and the third
for the press and propaganda. Double walls were to provide even
temperature. A gigantic spiral, which coiled around the entire
building, was the symbol of the new spirit of Communist dynamics
in contrast to the bourgeois horizontal, which was the symbol of
the spirit of greed. Steel and glass, materials created by fire, sym-
bolized the power of a sea of flame. The Palace of Labor was
conceived on an equally grand scale and was to be one hundred
meters long, with an aerodrome and radio station on the roof, and
a central hall that could accommodate eight thousand representatives of the world's toiling masses.

Naturally neither of these projects ever materialized, because
these grandiose plans were worked out with a total disregard for
building material, technical possibilities, or the purpose for which
the buildings were to serve. They had to be put aside when expert
architects undertook the work and from fantastic sketches proceeded to actual construction.

The problem Russian architects had to face was that of applying
engineering methods used in constructing bridges, elevators, and
factories to the building of dwelling houses. Architects abroad
scarcely ventured to do it. On the contrary, in building houses for
the working people on the outskirts of large cities they always
tried to make them look like individual units, in order to create,
if possible, the illusion of a real home. But the Communist views
on family life are well known. Their ideal—as yet not attained—
is to create a type of dwelling house fully adapted to the needs of
communal life. Thus for them the transition from a factory to a
private dwelling was much easier than for the architects of other
countries, because a similarity between the two buildings was
desired.

In the quest for a new style the first things to vanish were

all the decorative parts that had been inherited from the Baroque
—pillars, capitals, balustrades, broken pediments, etc. Only the
most indispensable parts in the structure of a house, the walls,
doors, and windows—the bare skeleton of the building—remained.
However, with the development of the American skyscraper, the
monotony has been broken by many divisions of walls and superimposed stories in a series of groups, systematically ascending
towards a central tower. This type of modern architecture allows
for the introduction of classical or even Gothic forms into it.

In Soviet Russia all disputes about modern architectural style
have as their chief theme the question whether it is admissible to
retain any connection with the past and use ornamental elements.
The radical trend of pure constructivism absolutely denies this possibility, and deems that the success or failure of a building depends
on the degree to which aestheticism is eliminated from its construction. A dwelling house is considered a success when the architect departs from the idea of family comfort and creates a type
more nearly adapted to communal life. The fight against bourgeois tendencies in the field of architecture has grown more intense
during recent years. Here the slogan "Bring art to the masses"
found expression in the command that "social elements" take an
active part in the discussions of architectural projects. Thus, in
1928 the *Komsomol Truth* demanded that there should be a public
discussion of the project for Lenin's Library and the house on
the banks of the Moskva River already under construction for the
Central Executive Committee and the Soviet of People's Commis-
sars. A public debate took place between Mordvinov, the leftist
architect, and the rightists, over the erection of the post office in
Kharkov; workmen interfered and with their arguments defeated
the supporters of "pillars in Indian, Egyptian, and other abstruse
styles." Mordvinov won the fight. However, here as in other fields,
Soviet architects have not been able to progress from a repudiation
of the "retrogressive, bourgeois tendencies" to positive achievements. In an article published in the *Almanac of Literature and
Art* a Soviet critic was forced to admit that as yet there did not
exist either a "united front of proletarian architects or a proletarian
style of architecture." "The left sector of architects is disintegrating

into a number of trends and schools warring with each other," and the only remedy he could suggest was "to place architecture under a strict social control."

Thus the ultimate outcome of the development of architecture in Soviet Russia was the same as that we have observed in both literature and painting.

V

MUSIC

I N passing to the history of Russian music, and in comparing
it with that of the West, we shall find in this field the same
parallelism in the development of general traits and the same
peculiarities of detail—at times very essential—that we found in
the history of painting and literature. Naturally here too, because
of the special conditions of national development, the differences
between Russia and the West were particularly great at the beginning of the Russian historical process, while with the approach
towards modern times they become gradually attenuated and
are replaced with a more and more clearly defined parallelism.

Western music was the product of a powerful cultural influence
exercised by the church on the primitive folk song. The Gregorian
church choral began by replacing the ancient five-tone scale of the
folk song, which had neither fourth nor seventh, with the classic
diatonic scale. Then, still within the confines of church music,
began the development of modern harmony. Folk song supplied
the melody; the medieval style of church music taught the accom-
paniment of consonant voices. Thus both monodic and polyphonic
styles were introduced into the music of modern times, and it
acquired systematized harmony. In Russia, in this case too, the
Church avoided ancient folk music, and for centuries church and
folk song existed side by side without in any way influencing each
other. In fact, the Church actually persecuted folk song. As late
as 1636, Patriarch Jehosophat ordered all Russian musical instruments burned at a solemn auto-da-fé in Moscow. The natural
outcome was that Russian folk song has retained its peculiar
rhythm and even its primitive scale until the present day, while

church music, through its seclusion, received no impetus from the outside and gave none to the laity. It remained for a long time as immobile, undeveloped, and monodic as it was when, as a part of the church service, it was brought to Russia either from Byzantium or the South Slavonic countries. Thus ancient Russia had no part in the development of the polyphonic style, which in the West paved the way for Palestrina and was nearing its final stage in the fifteenth century. Naturally Russia played no creative rôle in the further progress of Western music, when chromatics were added to the old diatonic scale and the ancient church modes were replaced by the modern major and minor. Therefore, in order to begin its own independent development, Russian music had to adopt the European technique, and only later, when that was mastered, did it find in the ancient Russian folk song its liberation from foreign shackles, and so was able to contribute its own national elements to the history of music.

Nevertheless, in the field of Russian church music, as in that of icon painting, there was a movement parallel with that of the West, though far more elementary.

Unfortunately it is very difficult to follow the progress of this movement, because the peculiar manner of writing music, which Russia, through the medium of the Southern Slavs, had adopted from the Greeks, complicates the study of the changes introduced by Russian singers. The earliest notation (*Kondakarny*) has not as yet been deciphered. All we know is that it preserved fully the wealth of the ancient Byzantine church music, which differed from the more modern one in that the continuous melody dominated the recitative while later it was just the opposite. Another notation now popularly known as *Znamenny* (semeionic from Greek *semeion* = sign), as written up to the fifteenth century, is even yet very little understood. The fact that this system of signs, later called "hooks" or "neumes," remained unchanged, testifies also to the changelessness of the music they represented. There were two reasons for this: first, sacred songs could not be changed because they constituted a part of the immutable divine service; and second, because in music the Byzantine achievements were so great that they were beyond the reach of the Russian people.

Moreover, those who transcribed the manuscripts did not understand the intricate signs, and in copying them they disfigured the neumatic writing. When in order to shorten the divine service the clergy introduced the custom of reading and singing several prayers simultaneously, the acme of confusion was reached. A contemporary describes the service as follows. "Two, three, or six people chant simultaneously without understanding what the other is saying, and the noise produced on both sides of the holy church by reading and singing is so great that no one can understand anything." But as long as the statutes and the text of the divine service remained unchanged and everything was read and sung as prescribed, the church was satisfied.

During the sixteenth century the early signs of an independent attitude toward what was being adopted manifested themselves in a protest against purely ritualistic views on the divine service. This led to various attempts at simplification of notation and even to the traditional monodic singing being accompanied by other voices. On this ground, as we have said, secular music in the West was successfully developed from sacred music, whereas in Russia, because of the complete ignorance of the theory of music, the disregard for folk songs, in which polyphony had already existed, and the unsatisfactory method of notation, the subject was confined, until the following period, to a few ineffectual efforts.

As a result of its ignorance and tardiness, in the second half of the seventeenth century Russia had to acquire from the West both the lineal notation and polyphonic choral singing. These innovations were introduced to Moscow by Kievan Russia, which had already adopted them from Poland. We know that all the contemporary influences both in literature and architecture came through the same channel. Up to the end of the eighteenth century the Ukrainian singers served as intermediaries in the assimilation of everything new in Western music. The early Russian reformer F. V. Rtishchev was so delighted with the polyphonic singing he had heard in Kiev that he had the choristers brought to his St. Andrew Monastery. Boiarin P. V. Sheremetev also had a number of Kievan singers and musicians at his home in Moscow. Paul of Aleppo has recounted that at the housewarming given by

Patriarch Nikon "both the Tsar and the Patriarch were very delighted with the singing of the Cossacks' children, brought from Poland by the Tsar as a gift to the Patriarch."

Judging by the following protest of Archpriest Avvakum, polyphonic singing must have gained favor rapidly. "In many of the churches at Moscow they sing songs instead of sacred chants, . . . wave their hands, shake their heads, and stamp their feet as do the Latin organists."

A far more important fact was that with the new style and method, music acquired also fresh themes. The profane style of Southeastern cantatas and psalms was introduced into the divine service. The Russian choristers lacked the skill and were not allowed to adapt ancient monodic melodies to the new style, and they accepted the new music, as they had accepted the old, without any change. Composers and theorists, following upon the singers, also came from the South, and one of them, N. P. Duletsky, a native of Lithuania, was made director of his Chapel of Singers by Tsar Theodore. He translated his *Idea on the Grammar of Music* (1679) from Polish into Russian and compiled a *Grammar of Musical Singing,* through which the Russians acquired a knowledge of the Italian school of the sixteenth and seventeenth centuries. Duletsky's pupils soon mastered the elementary forms and methods of the Western style, and so with no difficulty could compose polyphonic chants of twenty-four or even forty-eight voices which they divided into groups in order to obtain a contrast of sound and variety of tone.

The denationalization of the Church, and the fact that there were many immigrants from South Russia in the ranks of its clergy, undoubtedly accelerated the transition from the Orthodox ideographic notation to this new Western style, but even their patronage was unable to establish it in Russia. Under Peter the Great and his successors the adoptions in this field, as in other branches of culture, were no longer made through an intermediary, but from a direct source. Polyphonic singing paved the way for secular music, which with the first days of Peter's reform found free access into the country. At the courts of Peter's successors Italian music and particularly Italian opera came to the fore. It was initiated by the Empress Anna, who in 1735 invited the Italian composer Francesco Araja to produce at the theatre in the Palace his opera *La Forza dell' Amore e dell' Odio,* as translated by Trediakovsky, with the choir of the Imperial Chapel of Singers acting as a chorus. "These musical singers," wrote Staehlin, "have developed the taste for Italian music to such an extent that in their interpretation of the arias many of them equal the best Italian artists."

From that time on Russia attracted many outstanding Italian composers. Not only did Araja live there for twenty-eight years (1735–63) and produce seventeen operas, but Raupach (1735–64), Galuppi, Angelini (1768), Traetta (1775), Paesiello (1783–85), Cimarosa (1789–92), Sarti (1798), and Astariti (1794–1800) also lived there. French comic opera was imported into Russia, and the operatic repertory was enriched by the works of Monsigny, Philidor, Grétry, Dalayrac, Méhul, and others. Empress Elizabeth rewarded Razumovsky, an Ukrainian court chorister and bandore player, by marrying him. The Emperors Peter III and Paul I both played the violin. In the days of Catherine II, Gregory Teplov, a well-known statesman, excelled as composer, virtuoso, and conductor, and in 1768 he led an orchestra at the theatre in the Palace in which the Princess of Courland, two Naryshkin brothers, Count Stroganov, Senator Trubetskoy, Chamberlain Iaguzhinsky, and other "thrice-noble" musicians played.

The entire preparatory period in the history of Russian music was effaced and made to appear imitative by the rays of Glinka's fame. Nevertheless, in the history of music, as in those of painting and architecture, we discover several independent manifestations that gradually created the atmosphere in which Glinka's advent seems neither sudden nor inexplicable. It is interesting to record that the first Russian composers came from the lower social strata and that their works brought to the stage both Russian folk song and customs. Indeed, they no longer were compelled to adhere to a "serious" form of music but were allowed to compose light, short, comic operas, which towards the end of the eighteenth century became very popular, and to introduce in them folk song and dance. One of these composers, Michael Matinsky, a serf of Count S. P. Iaguzhinsky who sent him to travel and study in Italy, merits special attention. Upon his return Matinsky wrote an opera called *St. Petersburg Merchants' Row* (1779) which, though lacking

musical value, nevertheless became a tremendous success with the
public because of its popular content. In his opera Matinsky not
only introduced folk songs, but also the ceremony of the bride's
party on the eve of her marriage, and a musical characterization
of merchants soliciting patronage. As a composer Evstigney Fomin, the son of a simple gunner, was of far greater importance.
After receiving a primary education in music from Professor Buini,
who taught piano at the Academy of Arts, Fomin was sent to Italy
(1782–85) and obtained his academic diploma from Giambattista
Martini, the famous contrapuntist of Bologna, with whom Bere-
zovsky, the Russian composer of sacred songs, had studied at a
somewhat earlier date. Mattei, who also taught Rossini and Donizetti, was Fomin's second master. Thirty operas have been ascribed
to Fomin, but Finagin, a modern student, believes that there were
only ten, four of which are still extant: *The Valiant Novgorod
Knight Boeslaevich,* composed in 1786 at the command of Empress Catherine II, who had written the libretto; *Coachmen
at Relay* (1787); *Orpheus* (1792); and *Americans* (1800). In
Coachmen at Relay the songs and choral parts are combined me-
chanically, but the popular melodies are for the first time orchestrated without any disfiguring of their national peculiarities, while
in *Americans* and more especially in *Orpheus* the musical interpretation of the characters is rather good. *Orpheus,* Fomin's opera
of "lofty style," deals with a subject that was previously used
both by Monteverde and Gluck and is written in the form of
melodic recitative. The orchestration is simple but expressive and
in harmony with the subject. In the free and artistic transmutation
of the Russian folk song the national character is already beginning
to be felt, and marks the transition to Glinka's works.

It is important to point out that, notwithstanding the lack of
improvement in the quality of music, the interest in it and the
means for its study increased. In the first half of the nineteenth
century there already existed a long list of foreign operas translated into Russian and sung by a Russian cast. The public became
familiar with Cherubini (1834), Mozart (1816–28), Rossini (1822),
Weber (1829), and Herold (1834). In 1835–36 Meyerbeer's *Rob-
ert le Diable,* Rossini's *Semiramis,* and Bellini's *Romeo and Juliet*
were presented by Russian artists. Cavos and Verstovsky com-

posed operas in the Russian style, and although these works were forgotten after the appearance of Glinka, they were nevertheless far more advanced than those of the eighteenth century. In the meantime symphonic and concert music was also developed, and in 1802 the first Philharmonic Society was formed in St. Petersburg. It was there that the French conductor Paris led performances of Haydn, Mozart, Handel, and Beethoven; Rode and Field made their appearances, and Catalani won her laurels. Many of the nobles had private orchestras made up of their serfs; the number of amateurs increased rapidly, and by 1822–23 there were in St. Petersburg twenty qualified professors and women teachers of music, and forty music shops. In fact, there developed a musical set and atmosphere due to which music as a profession was no longer confined to the lower classes but soon brought to professionals of the wealthy and privileged class, if not an income, at least honor and fame.

We shall now pass to the period in the history of Russian music which may be called "classical." Glinka's (1804–57) appearance marks the same stage in the history of music as that of Pushkin in the history of literature.[1] They each inaugurated a period of independent creation at a time when the old epoch of imitativeness had not yet become history, and consequently they were both equally misunderstood. Music and literature had just begun to free themselves of court patronage, but the new surroundings were still not congenial. Neither the composer nor the author had yet found their public; they had to be satisfied with friendly salons, or seek the patronage of the mighty. In music, because of the greater complications of a public performance, the feeling of dependence continued longer than it did in literature. This fact is clearly evidenced in Glinka's fate. As in the case of Pushkin, the standing of the artist among his contemporaries cannot restrain us, while speaking in retrospect, from placing Glinka's name at the head of the classical period of national Russian music.

Neither the indications that Glinka depended on foreign composers, nor the accusations of modern professionals that he was amateurish, can change our opinion on this subject. True, Glinka lived at a time when in other countries a national movement in

_____

[1] See Part II, ch. 2.—ED.

music had begun, and Weber had been acclaimed in Germany, but Glinka only met his famous contemporaries, Liszt, Berlioz, and Meyerbeer, at a later date. The idea of composing a national opera occurred to him not from a desire to imitate these composers, but because during his trip abroad in 1830–34 he felt that the Italian ideas were alien to his own. "Everything I have composed to please the people of Milan has proved to me that I was on the wrong path and that I could never honestly be Italian. Nostalgia gradually gave me the idea of composing in Russian," Glinka wrote in his notes, adding in explanation of his idea on the Russian style,

It was an arduous task trying to imitate the Italian *sentimento brillante,* as they call the sense of well-being which results from their natures being happily developed under the influence of the beneficent southern sun. We, people of the north, are different: we are either unmoved by impressions or they are engraved in our hearts; we feel either unrestrained joy or we shed bitter tears. In Russia, love, elsewhere a happy and vivifying emotion, always contains a tinge of sadness. No doubt our mournful song is the child of the north or perhaps was transmitted to us by the people of the Orient, whose song is equally plaintive even in happy Andalusia.

Here is the first indication that Russian folk song was to be the cardinal element in Glinka's works. This and the five-months' course in the theory of music which he took under Professor Dehn in Berlin on his way back to Russia, comprise all Glinka's resources. In his national opera *A Life for the Tsar* he combined the three elements: Russian folk song, Italian roulades, and German harmony and orchestration. Nevertheless Berlioz and Chaikovsky acknowledged that Glinka's opera was "truly national, original, having no prototype or antecedent," and a work which placed him among the "most outstanding composers of his time." Yet it was the same Chaikovsky who, admitting that *A Life for the Tsar* "in its genius, spirit, novelty, and irreproachable technique ranked among the greatest and deepest creations of art," was never reconciled to Glinka's amateurishness, which he ascribed to the effect of his surroundings.

The success of *A Life for the Tsar* was due largely to its plot, for the choice of which Glinka was personally thanked by the Emperor, and to its title, which made it appropriate for official representations ón imperial fete days. It was introduced to the public in 1836, the same year as Bruellow's painting,[2] and because at that period everything national was officially encouraged both works were promptly included in the list of great national creations. As to the merits of the music in Glinka's opera, the public appreciated only its tunefulness, while its popular element aroused profound contempt from the aristocrats who said that it was "music for coachmen." Verstovsky's opera, *Tomb of Askold,* which had been produced the year before, because of its less complicated technique and greater action appealed far more to the general public. Six years later the breach between Glinka and his audience grew even wider, for it was during that period that the composer first disapproved definitely of the Italian manner; he was now "dissatisfied with the existing musical system" in general, and found that "music needed to be invigorated and refreshed through the medium of other elements"; and so in *Ruslan and Liudmila* (1842) he put his new ideas into practice. This time, while the public liked the scenery and costumes designed by Bruellow, it was disappointed with the libretto, and particularly puzzled with the new and strange musical subtleties, so that the opera was almost a complete failure. According to Bulgarin's malicious review in the *Northern Bee:*

Everybody went to the theatre prejudiced in favor of the composer and with an ardent desire to contribute to his triumph, but they came away as from a funeral! The first words heard on everyone's lips were "how *boring.*" Does it mean that the audience has not understood the music of *Ruslan and Liudmila?* Assuming this were so, for whom then are the operas composed? For the learned contrapuntists, for musical experts, and composers, or the public, the masses? Music composed to be immortal and for posterity should be kept in a portfolio, and the public given only that which it is able to grasp and to feel.

Even Glinka's friends were of the same opinion, and the opera was withdrawn from the repertory at the end of the first season and

[2] See above, ch. 2.—ED.

did not make its reappearance for twenty-one years. This so mortified Glinka that he went abroad, only to convince himself once
again, after his success in Paris, that "his soul was Russian." There
is a parallel between Glinka and Pushkin, whose *Boris Godunov*
also had had a cold reception. Both failures were due to the back-
wardness of the Russian public which, being led by the court,
reverted to simple music, and the following season in St. Petersburg the Italian opera celebrated one of its most brilliant triumphs.

There was scarcely any change in the situation when Dargomyzhsky (1813–69), another "gentleman dilettante" with novel
ideas, decided to work on the development of Russian opera. "In
my opinion," he wrote in 1853, "Glinka has developed only the
lyrical in opera. His dramatic element is too monotonous and his
comedy is not national. . . . I am working assiduously on our
native dramatic moments in my *Rusalka* [Water Sprite]." This
was achieved by melodic recitative. It is true that Glinka concen-
trated all his attention on the musical score and only when it was
finished did he allow someone to write the libretto. This is particularly noticeable in *Ruslan and Liudmila,* where the greatest
stress is placed upon the orchestral and vocal ensembles, while action is of secondary importance. But to Dargomyzhsky an opera
had to be opera, i. e., words had to be as important as the music.
This, of course, lent to his compositions greater realism. Yet his
idea too was misunderstood at first. *Rusalka,* carelessly produced in
1856, was not sufficiently appreciated by the public, and late in 1857
Dargomyzhsky wrote:

My position in St. Petersburg as an artist is not an enviable one.
The majority of our amateurs and newspaper scribblers do not
think I am inspired. Their unimaginative ear demands melody, and
that is not my object. I have no intention of lowering the level of
music to entertainment in order to suit them. *I want sounds to
express words directly*. But this is beyond their comprehension.

The words italicized comprised the program of the national
school of music. Russian music followed the movement that prevailed between the eighteen-sixties and eighties in all other
branches of art, and strove to be realistic. Therefore, when in 1866
Rusalka was again produced, Dargomyzhsky admitted that it had

"a fabulous, even mystifying, success," and explained the mystery as being the "work of time." In the meantime what exactly had happened that was new?

Rusalka was founded on a national theme which corresponded to the new mood, and besides that, during these years the amateurs and musical salons in Russia had been replaced by a musical set with a developed and serious professional interest in everything modern in the way of music. This was followed by something as yet unknown in Russian music—a strife among the various trends.

A. N. Serov (1820–71), the first qualified Russian musical critic, was a very characteristic figure of the intermediate period between amateurism and professionalism. With his brusqueness and passion for polemics he incurred the animosity of the two schools at that time in the process of formation—the European, or academic, which originated in the conservatories founded by the Rubinstein brothers,[3] and the Russian, which was still semi-amateurish. V. V. Stasov (1824–1906), who had been Serov's closest friend ever since their student days at the School of Law, became his bitterest enemy in championing the cause of the Russian school of music. Stasov praised the followers of Glinka, while Serov scorned the ambitions of this "mighty band" and voiced his great admiration for Wagner, ardently patronizing his appearances in Russia. Nevertheless, in composing *Judith* (1863), which brought him fame at the age of forty-three, and *Rogneda* (1865), Serov did not attempt to imitate his idol, but strove after Meyerbeer's superficial achievements, which were more suitable to his musical training. As is often the case with those expert in the history of their own particular branch of art or science, Serov was and consciously wanted to be an eclectic. He expressed the hope that the "Slavonic school would soon come into existence," and thought himself "justified in expecting that within it would be combined eclectically all that was best in its predecessors: . . . the dramatic truth . . . of the French and German schools, . . . the Italian tunefulness and purity of melody, and the serious, intellectual, and profound development of counterpoint as found in the German school —all this to meet under especial conditions of individuality emanating from a musical soil new and virginal." *En musique on doit*

[3] Anton (1829–94) and Nicholas (1835–81).—ED.

être cosmopolite, Serov had written to Stasov during the years of their youth and friendship.

The Russian school of music, which derived its origin from Glinka, was destined to acquire a definite form under some of his younger contemporaries, whom Serov had refused to recognize. It was indeed a "special and individual" school, but by no means an eclectic one. Simultaneously with the Russian school and side by side with it, there was also founded a truly cosmopolitan school under the serious instruction of Anton Rubinstein at the Russian Musical Society in St. Petersburg (1862), and of his brother Nicholas in Moscow (1866). Serov, who had been ignored by the Rubinsteins, rebelled against this school, called it anti-national, and went so far as to say that no knowledge of music could be acquired under academic instruction, after which it became the fashion to belittle the importance of this so-called "cosmopolitan" movement. Thus the genius of Anton Rubinstein, the first Russian artist to be acclaimed abroad, was applauded only as a pianist, while his numerous compositions were considered of secondary importance, except for *The Demon,* which was produced at the Russian opera. This, however, cannot prevent us from recognizing that the works of Rubinstein not only have their value as scholarly reproductions of the old classics and romanticists ("academism"), but also have a definite individuality, melodic inventiveness, and even tinges of nationality, based on the adoption of the Oriental element, to which other Russian composers frequently resorted. But of course the chief value of the Rubinstein brothers to Russian music lies in their vast and important task of spreading really professional education throughout Russia. In this sense the opening up of high-grade musical schools at the capitals marked an era in the history of Russian music.

This circumstance naturally did not end the strife taking place between the national element and cosmopolitanism, but on the contrary only aggravated it. In the heat of this controversy Chaikovsky (1840–93), the most outstanding pupil of the St. Petersburg Conservatory and a real professional, who after his graduation in 1865 became professor at the Moscow Conservatory, was also called a cosmopolite. Although he wrote music treasured the world over, which has outlived him and found a permanent place in cosmopolitan classical music, nevertheless the national spontaneity of feeling and the sincerity of its expression remained the essential parts of Chaikovsky's compositions. It was characteristic of him that this feeling proved to be profoundly sad and plaintive—such as the people abroad were accustomed to recognize as the "Russian soul." Chaikovsky did not introduce modern ideas in his music, and profiting thereby his enemies accused him of academism. But he possessed a style of his own, not only profoundly individual but autobiographic, for the creation of which he made use of every contemporary technique and coloring. Was Chaikovsky a Romanticist? The answer depends on one's definition of Romanticism. If it includes the lyrical and emotional in music, then Chaikovsky was a Romanticist, for he was both lyrical and emotional. But we are accustomed to think of Romanticism as tending towards a world of unreality and mysticism, and Chaikovsky possessed none of these traits; like the times he was rather realistic, and interpreted emotions as vividly as he felt them. At least he was never tearful or sentimental, as his enemies accused him of being, because his feelings were sincere and towards the end of his life even tragic. These very characteristics made his Russian soul a human one and understood by all mankind, and in spite of the accusations brought forward by the "refined" and "satiated" they secured him the love of the masses, which still continue to crowd the theatres and concert halls to hear *Eugene Onegin* and the Sixth Symphony.

We shall now pass to another trend, which regarded itself as representative in Russian music of the national tradition as inaugurated by Glinka. After 1859 a few composers who, like Serov, had had no systematic training and who therefore had been called "dilettanti," became intimate friends of Dargomyzhsky and *habitués* at his parties. Among them were Cui (1835–1918) and Musorgsky (1839–81), two young officers, and Balakirev (1837–1910), lately graduated from the university; somewhat later, in the early sixties, a naval cadet, subsequently naval officer, Rimsky-Korsakov (1844–1908), and Borodin (1834–87), a young professor of chemistry. Balakirev, the most erudite, soon became the acknowledged head of the circle, the members of which he in turn initiated into the mysteries of musical technique. There was no lack of talent and zeal in the circle, and the youthful enthusiasm of its members was strengthened by the fact that as pioneers of the "Russian" school of music they found themselves opposed to the professional "cosmopolitanism" of the Conservatory. Although in the opinion of the public and the critics the latter occupied a dominating position, the Balakirev circle never considered laying down its arms. On the contrary, under the leadership of V. V. Stasov, its enthusiastic supporter, it courageously attacked the enemy. In the same year (1862) that the Conservatory was opened in St. Petersburg, the young musicians founded their own Free School of Music, and its concerts, conducted by Balakirev, became exhibitions of the works of modern Russian composers, whose motto was realism. Musorgsky, the most brilliant member of the new school, carried realism in music even further than Dargomyzhsky. It was not without cause that Musorgsky sympathized with Gogol and Nekrasov, and that in his zeal for exposing the evils of the day he was likened to Perov. "The artistic representation of nothing but beauty in a material sense," he said, "is crude childishness, art in its infancy. The finest traits of human nature and human masses . . . untouched by anyone, . . . the assiduous exploration of these unknown regions and their conquest, are the call of a true artist." Faithful to this call Musorgsky, with unprecedented daring, made music speak and depict indignation, suffering, and laughter, peasant life, the wooing of a half-wit, the sorrowful chant of an orphan beggar, and the psychology of a child at play; he even composed musical caricatures, while his musical satire rose to scourging sarcasm against the contemporary representatives of formalism in music. No other member of the circle ever dared come so dangerously near the truth. Subsequently Cui condemned it as a violation of the rules of art, while in his rearrangement of *Boris Godunov* Rimsky-Korsakov tried to soften Musorgsky's most salient audacities.

Musorgsky's two immortal operas—*Boris Godunov* and *Khovanshchina*—represent the composer's talent at its prime and at the same time prove his loyalty to the trend he had chosen. Both themes enabled him to unfold great pictures of two momentous periods in Russia's historic past.[4] Music served only as a frame for the realistic content. Musorgsky wished to have a clear idea of the events and conditions of life during these remote periods, so with Stasov's assistance he studied all the authentic documents in detail. It took him five and a half years, from the autumn of 1869 to the spring of 1874, to compose *Boris Godunov*. He began *Khovanshchina* in 1872, and with interruptions worked on it until June 16, 1881, when he died at the age of forty-two. The works of Karamzin and Pushkin supplied the composer with the plot for *Boris Godunov*, but Musorgsky was not satisfied with merely following these sources. It is superfluous to speak of the exceptional gift for musical characterization which helped this composer reveal to the audience the soul of his heroes, for indeed his realism was not reduced to naturalism. On this subject Rimsky-Korsakov said that Musorgsky did not require a *leitmotif* in order to define his hero, but produced a living man with all a man's emotions. What Musorgsky made use of to enrich the subject was no less characteristic. The vivid reënactment of the social surroundings, in which Pushkin's chronicle unfolded itself on the stage, was most striking, and it is almost impossible to enumerate the typical traits which Musorgsky adopted directly from historical source material. The broad treatment of popular scenes is particularly characteristic and justifies his calling his operas "popular dramas." Musorgsky showed unusual perspicacity and tact when treating the psychology of the masses. Whereas the ideology of the eighteen-sixties and seventies demanded a blind admiration of the masses, Musorgsky presented them on the stage as they were in reality without the slightest idealization, yet with a feeling of deep sympathy and understanding of the soul of the people.

Khovanshchina gave the composer an even wider scope for revealing his talent and the spirit of the times. The conflict of two cultures, the old and the new, that of the people and that of

---

[4] The action in *Boris Godunov* takes place during the Time of Troubles, in the early seventeenth century. *Khovanshchina* deals with the struggle between the Old Ritualists and the adherents of Western innovations during the early years of Peter the Great's reign.—ED.

Peter, and its profound tragedy ending in a terrible scene with the self-immolation of the Old Ritualists,[5] supplied vast material for both musical characterization and scenery. The delay in the composition of the opera was due in part to the impossibility of including all the accumulated material in the confines of a scenic production. The difficulty was that the opera had no hero, only social sets and popular masses, which weakened the dramatic interest. But Musorgsky showed great artistic sense by introducing the moral and spiritual tragedy of Martha, the Old Ritualist, into this variegated texture of human relations.

Both these wonderful works brought the composer nothing but grief. *Boris Godunov* was not accepted by the Imperial theatre until it had been rearranged, and then, along with the public's acclaim, it provoked the disapproval of Musorgsky's friends and a frankly malevolent criticism from Cui. Some were annoyed with the musical daring of the "arrogant" composer, while others complained that Russia was represented in too dark a color, but to the composer's indignation all demanded "beauty in the music," which for the most part they were unable to detect. Musorgsky never saw his *Khovanshchina* produced or heard it played by the orchestra. At the time of his death he had only finished a piano score and orchestrated a few scenes. He was not understood until long after his death, and even then his posthumous fame was not based on what he regarded as his greatest achievement. While the conception of beauty in music underwent the change he had desired, Musorgsky the realist was not fully appreciated. This realistic psychologist was represented as a mystic even by those who recognized him. They based their belief on the fact that during his last years Musorgsky, under the stress of sad experiences, thought, spoke, and sang more of death than of life which he so loved and desired. We shall return again to Musorgsky in connection with a posthumous revival of his works.

Other members of the circle, less erratic and bohemian than the creator of *Boris Godunov* and *Khovanshchina,* though not endowed with equally great individual talent, have succeeded nevertheless in leaving a mark in the history of Russian music. We shall not enlarge on Balakirev, the theorist of the group, or César Cui,

---

[5] On the Old Ritualists and the practice of self-immolation, see Part I, ch. 3.—Ed.

the musical critic of the circle who propagated program music and recitative in the opera, and composed graceful songs and eight operas that have been entirely forgotten. A. P. Borodin was a greater musician, for he was equally the master of symphonic, chamber, and operatic music. His famous opera *Prince Igor* was finished after his sudden death in 1887 by Rimsky-Korsakov in collaboration with A. K. Glazunov (1865-1936). In its realistic popular scenes and its recitative element *Prince Igor* upheld the traditions of the circle. However, Borodin no longer avoided arias, and protested against the "purely recitative style," preferring *cantabile* and placing the vocal parts above the orchestra. The Oriental element in his music is common to other Russian composers; the importance placed upon this element actually created the erroneous impression abroad that Oriental melody and harmony were peculiar to Russian music. Finally, it must be pointed out that in the critics' opinion Borodin possessed a characteristic in common with Glinka, for his music was also objective, i. e., Borodin was able to withhold his own moods from his heroes, thus making them more striking and individual.

N. A. Rimsky-Korsakov lived longer and was more prolific than all the members of the circle, and it was natural that in his works the further evolution of Russian music found a more complete expression. He took an active part in this development, while among his pupils were some of the most talented representatives of the next generation of Russian composers. Like others of the circle, which he had joined in 1861 as its fourth member, Rimsky-Korsakov for a long time remained an amateur, but he soon outdistanced his friends by composing a symphony—the first Russian one to achieve great success when played at the concert in the Free School of Music. The symphony was followed by such important works as *Sadko,* a "musical picture" (1866), *Antar,* another symphony (1868), and finally by the opera *Pskovitianka* (1868-71). Even among others aside from the members of the circle, who composed only during their leisure moments, Rimsky-Korsakov's capacity for work was exceptional, and yet the young composer was never satisfied with his achievements and strove always for more. He rapidly outgrew the circle, and immediately following the completion of *Pskovitianka,* he underwent a radical change, which was to play a significant part in the further development of the history of Russian music. A. K. Glazunov gave the following account of this change: "At that time there existed a fallacy that a free artist had no need to study. Rimsky-Korsakov did not share this opinion, and when composing *Pskovitianka* he complained bitterly to me that his hands were tied, that his aspirations were greater than his achievements. This fact weighed heavily upon him and he decided to learn the technique of composition. That necessitated his studying harmony, counterpoint, and the fugue intently," particularly as he was offered (1871) the vacant chair of composition and orchestration at the St. Petersburg Conservatory. Chaikovsky was profoundly stirred when in 1875 Rimsky-Korsakov sent him some fruits of his exercises in these "musical artifices," and was only apprehensive that this novice in technique should become too zealous and develop into a "dull pedant." Indeed, there is over-abundance of technique in the Third Symphony (1875), as in a number of other contemporary works, but a collection of Russian folk songs published by Rimsky-Korsakov at that same time brought him much nearer the national source of Russian music. After this he revised all his previous compositions, and also with renewed ardor applied his knowledge to composing in a new manner and to the rearrangement of Dargomyzhsky, Borodin, and Musorgsky's unfinished works. *May Night* (1878) and especially *Snegurochka* (Snow-Maiden, 1880), which took him only a few months to compose, were examples of the greatness of his achievements and marked his transformation into a devotee of the Russian folk song. "I am ashamed to admit that I was jealous," Chaikovsky wrote after hearing *Snegurochka*. At that same period the most perfect of Rimsky-Korsakov's symphonic compositions, such as *Spanish Capriccio, Sheherazade,* and *Easter Sunday* also appeared. The last-named composition was the result of the new position, that of assistant manager of the Imperial Chapel of Singers, which Rimsky-Korsakov received in 1883 and which led him to study music of the Orthodox church, thus paving the way for the peerless *Legend of the City of Kitezh.*

It is impossible, and not necessary for our purpose, to analyze Rimsky-Korsakov's creative genius after his musical individuality had once been definitely established, and we shall only point out the chief characteristics of his works during the period of its full perfection. We must mention here that Rimsky-Korsakov was often compared to Wagner. Indeed, beginning with *Snegurochka* he more and more frequently recurred to a *leitmotif* for the characterization of his heroes, and like Wagner he chose his subjects almost exclusively from the national folklore, related to the legendary past when reality and fiction merged into an animistic conception of nature.

It continued so until Rimsky-Korsakov finally abandoned the forms of the old opera, with its arias and acts divided into solo numbers and ensembles, and, like Wagner, passed to uninterrupted action, where the unfolding of events and moods was expressed by the orchestra, while the part of the singers was confined to recitative. From a purely musical point of view it must be admitted that the broad treatment of the orchestra, the astonishing brilliance of complex instrumentation, and the bacchanal of sound, unknown to the old school, were gaining strength, and were the peculiar traits that made Rimsky-Korsakov so tremendously popular abroad.

However, besides the traits he had in common with Wagner, this composer had his own, absolutely Russian characteristics. Rimsky-Korsakov's recitative, with its uninterrupted interpretation by the orchestra, was not the foundation for musical construction, and the *leitmotif* therefore was not the chief factor. Even more important was the fact that Russian folklore, songs, *byliny,* sacred verse, popular legends, and tales did not attain the level of philosophical generalization, nor did they pretend to explain the history of mankind and the world. With Rimsky-Korsakov all these elements retained the artlessness of folklore, and that is why, instead of exalted inspirations, lyrical ecstasies, and profound dramatic conflicts, the theme of a tale was unfolded either in a satirical vein or in the form of an artistic miniature, as in *Tsar Saltan* or in *Le Coq d'or.* The tragedy of *Snegurochka* or the adventures of *Sadko* aroused the emotions of the audience but did not stir its mental powers, which was precisely what the change in public taste required. Because his music was too closely connected with the ideologic content of the drama, Wagner was

repudiated by the younger generation, whose new demands were
for less ideology and philosophy and a more humorous attitude
towards the theme, which had to be remote from reality. Rimsky-
Korsakov possessed this gift, he also accepted some new ideas in
harmony and thus was able to retain his connection with the
later generation and to found a school which in fact was quite
independent of the outmoded Balakirev circle.

We must add, however, that there is one exception in the works
of Rimsky-Korsakov. Apart from his humorous and fantastic
operas he composed the *Legend of the City of Kitezh,* a work with
roots reaching into the national tradition, which approaches the
psychology of the people from a different, a spiritually religious
side and produces a deep emotion that reminds one of Wagner's
Parsifal although quite foreign to its suffering and mysticism. But
in his fantastic and fairy-tale works Rimsky-Korsakov always remained a cheerful realist, and his audience scarcely had time to
accept the blending together of the fantastic and real worlds before he transformed mystery into an artistic skit.

After all that has been said it is not surprising that in the field
of music we cannot draw such a distinct line between the generations as Merezhkovsky's manifesto did in literature [6] and the appearance of *The World of Art* in the figurative arts. The children
were too closely bound by the teaching of the fathers to revolt
either against their ideology or their methods. Let us review the entire situation. From 1882 to 1892 Chaikovsky ruled supreme on the
operatic stage. After his death the legacy passed to Rimsky-Korsakov, who reconciled the Balakirev circle with the Conservatory.
Following the death of Rimsky-Korsakov (1908) the scepter of
the Conservatory and the musical world passed on to Glazunov.
Although they looked upon Glazunov as being too academic,
the younger generation still admired him as the last Russian
classicist, a supporter of pure music, who protested against any
romantic mixture of types and who composed instrumental music.
Thus, thanks to the vigor, brilliance, depth, and productiveness of
Rimsky-Korsakov, and Glazunov's gift for composition, the revolt was postponed for several decades, and then it was not mani-

[6] See Part II, ch. 3.—ED.

fested by an entire school, such as the Balakirev circle, but found only individual expression.

A. N. Skriabin (1872–1915) was one of these individual rebels. His psychology and ideology closely resemble those of the aesthetes of the early twentieth century; but as compared to actual modern music, his innovations are as artificial as those of Richard Strauss in comparison to Wagner. Sabaneiev, the critic, who was an intimate friend of Skriabin, described him as having been from early youth "delicate, effeminate, high-strung, self-confident, and prematurely sensual; erotic emotions were familiar to him when still a child, which explains the very great voluptuousness of his tone." Skriabin left the Cadet School after only four years of study; consequently he lacked a proper education. His works testify both to the great power he possessed as an artist and to his naïveté as a thinker. His notes contain a series of futile efforts at formulating a philosophical conception of himself as the center of creation. Skriabin's philosophizing friends supported his idea of the "Mystery"—an extraordinary and final creative effort in which there was to be no audience but all were to be performers. The composer never had time to write the "Mystery," for he died in 1915, yet he approached the idea in *Prométhée, Le Divin Poème,* and *Le Poème de l'extase.* Of course these orchestral compositions of Skriabin have musical value, but he attained the highest perfection in his works for the piano.

After Wagner in the West and Rimsky-Korsakov in Russia every musical work seemed but a brilliant imitation of new ideas. This explains why Skriabin, in spite of his great talent and the originality of his achievements in harmony, found himself in an impasse, gained no recognition outside of Russia, and did not influence the further progress of twentieth-century music. He had to cede the rôle of forerunner of new music to the representatives of younger generations (Skriabin was born in 1871, Stravinsky in 1882, and Prokofiev in 1891).

But here again we approach the moment when, like painting, Russian music became cosmopolitan without, however, losing its national character. Coming in touch with the newest Western trends, Russian music was not satisfied to imitate them, but in a

daring effort it tried to surpass them, and for a time succeeded in
becoming a source of imitation for Europe.

Up to the end of the nineteenth century Russian music was, so
to speak, provincial. Its very isolation from the course of progress
in Western music helped it to acquire a national character and to
create such valuable works that, when later the relations with the
outside world were established, they proved to be of universal importance. Musical language, as opposed to literary language, is
international, and unlike figurative arts can be easily transposed
and reproduced in many copies. But it only lives during the few
moments of its production. Thus, although music is more easily
internationalized than any other art, it is more difficult for a musical work to obtain lasting international approval and it lapses
sooner into oblivion. From this point of view we shall now examine
what the Russian composers adopted from international music
and what they added to it.

We know that Glinka, the founder of the national Russian
school, was subject to foreign influences, though when he came in
touch with them he was always conscious of feeling particularly
Russian. The chief obstacle in those days to the development of a
national independence in music was the imitation of Italian methods, and Glinka, who originally was fascinated by the Italians,
deliberately changed his attitude towards them and began to
compose in a different manner. His first opera nevertheless bore
marked traces of the Italian influence. That Glinka depended also
on the Germans is proved by the fact that five musical notebooks
of Professor Dehn, with whom he had studied in Berlin, remained
his chief manual of harmony until the last. During this same period
(1833–34) these five small musical notebooks were also carefully
copied by another novice, Dargomyzhsky. Both these composers
traveled abroad repeatedly and so had the opportunity to study the
new Western music at its very source and to meet its exponents.
In 1830, when in Germany, Glinka heard *Der Freischuetz* and
Fidelio, and in Italy met Donizetti, Bellini, and Mendelssohn.
Later he met Liszt in St. Petersburg (1842–43) and Berlioz in
Paris (1844). It was often said that Glinka's orchestration resembled that of Berlioz, in fact he himself admitted that the latter
"made a deep impression" on him. Berlioz, in his turn, placed

Glinka "in the first rank of outstanding composers," recognized in him "a great master of harmony" and spoke of his orchestration as having "the most modern and vital tone of our time." He added, moreover, that Glinka unquestionably possessed "an original inventiveness for melody" (article in the *Journal des Débats*). Nevertheless Glinka preferred the less cultured Spain to any other European country, and he brought the tunes of its national dances to Russia. He did not approve of Liszt's playing, and showed enthusiasm for the already outmoded compositions of Gluck, when he heard them for the first time in 1847. From that time on Glinka studied Gluck's scores most carefully and never parted from them. During Glinka's last stay in Berlin, Professor Dehn succeeded in arousing his interest in Bach and seventeenth-century church compositions, thereby separating him definitely from all connection with modern music. Glinka was terrified by Weber's dominant seventh, he never learned to appreciate Schumann, while Mozart and Beethoven in his opinion had "stolen from Gluck unmercifully." All this is characteristic of Glinka's outlook on music, which even for those days was limited.

Glinka's successors had still less connection outside of Russia than he had, for at that time began the estrangement from the West which soon changed into open antagonism: youth wished to become independent. Dargomyzhsky made two trips abroad (1844 and 1864), but his attitude towards modern European music remained rather disdainful and he hated Western customs, especially those of Paris. He received a cool welcome at Leipsic and Paris, and the ovations tendered him at Brussels were unable to dispel his natural indifference to European fame, and yet Dargomyzhsky nevertheless insisted that Berlioz be invited to Russia. But the Western innovators had already progressed further and, at that time, were led by Wagner, of whom Dargomyzhsky had only a very superficial knowledge. The progressive tendencies of the "mighty band"—even when they agreed with Wagner—developed along independent lines, and the composer of "Rusalka's melodious recitative" found the melodies of *Tannhaeuser* artificial and its harmony showing "morbid traits." On the Russian stage, realism and truth were expressed by quite different methods. *The Stone Guest,* the opera Dargomyzhsky composed just before his death (1868), became the new artistic testament for the members of the "mighty band," while it was not fully appreciated by the public until a much later date.

In Serov, Russia had a highly educated critic well versed in modern music. His object was to prove that the Russian national school was provincial and to retrieve Russian music from its isolation. As a youth his first infatuation was *Der Freischuetz,* but even at school he was well acquainted with the symphonies of Beethoven, then little known in Russia, Mozart, and the works of such modern composers as Schumann and Chopin. Then Weber and Schubert became gradually young Serov's favorites, but Meyerbeer, *"le favori de mon âme*—notwithstanding his falsity," soon became their rival. The appearance of Liszt in St. Petersburg during 1842 was to Serov "an event of world-wide importance." On his first trip abroad Serov heard *Tannhaeuser* and was fascinated with Wagner, whose theoretical compositions had been known to him since 1853. He met Liszt again in Weimar and with a growing intimacy he became absolutely captivated both by his playing and his compositions. At Baden-Baden Serov added another star to this constellation, in recognizing that in the domain of orchestral color Berlioz was the master of both Liszt and Wagner. During the meeting with his old idol Meyerbeer, Serov became convinced that, "as was to be expected, he equally hated with all his heart the entire new movement and Wagner's music." In the following year Serov heard *Tristan und Isolde* and *Lohengrin;* then he met Wagner personally and was definitely won over to his methods.

When, having absorbed the new ideas, Serov returned to Russia and found his friend and schoolmate V. Stasov ardently supporting the national Russian school, they naturally became bitter enemies. But neither did his admiration of Wagner find support at the Conservatory, which Rubinstein had lately opened. In such conditions Serov's extensive foreign experience found no immediate application in Russia. He sought solace in writing venomous articles, which brought him fame as a critic, but definitely severed his relations with the musical world. His operas were not sufficiently great to justify his written advocacy of modern methods and cosmopolitanism in music. The acclaim which *Judith* and

Rogneda received from the public should not be ascribed to Serov's admiration of Wagner, whom the Russian public was not yet able to appreciate, but to that secret love of Meyerbeer which he professed in his youth and to which in his works he always remained true. Indeed, it was due to Serov's efforts that *Lohengrin* was produced at the Imperial Opera in St. Petersburg, yet in spite of the enthusiastic reports which he sent Wagner after the performance, the opera was withdrawn from the repertory. In a word, Serov's propaganda of cosmopolitanism in music was too premature to be successful. But was the Russian public sufficiently mature for the "national school"?

The story of the "mighty band," as mentioned above, can best answer this question. At the time the "mighty band" was formed, there already existed in Russian music a certain national tradition. At the musicales, which its members first gave in Dargomyzhsky's home and subsequently at that of their leader Balakirev, the young musicians worshiped Glinka. The "mighty band" regarded Bach as a "musical fossil," Haydn and Mozart as "antiquated," and Beethoven, except for his Ninth Symphony and last quartets, "outmoded." Schumann was most popular with them, and they deigned also to approve of Chopin, but they accused Liszt of being theatrical, while Wagner was never even mentioned. Such was the mood of the small group of skilled amateurs at the beginning of the eighteen-sixties, when the leadership in musical education was assumed by the Rubinsteins' Conservatory. Anton Rubinstein had just returned from his first triumphal tour in Europe and was preparing himself for more extensive ones both in Europe and America. He could well have broadened the musical horizon of the national school, but he chose to ignore its members and they responded with sarcasm to his neglect. However, the Conservatory attended to its duties and, being patronized by many wealthy and influential people, it soon gained public approval. The "mighty band" had neither powerful nor wealthy patrons, but its spirit of opposition to everything old and its exclusiveness in the desire to develop a style of its own increased during the sixties. Balakirev, the school's exacting mentor, was the first to experience the result of this estrangement from the public taste. His Free School of Music and its symphony concerts could not compete with those of the Conservatory. At the beginning of the seventies, resenting the public's lack of interest, Balakirev secluded himself and gradually became an odd type of mystic, a somber pessimist, and a real burden to himself and those about him. Cui, Borodin, and Rimsky-Korsakov, annoyed with Balakirev's dictatorship, deserted him, and in 1875 the "mighty band" ceased to exist. Borodin gives us a vivid description of the situation.

I think the course of events is a perfectly natural one. As long as we were under the wings of the brood hen (I mean Balakirev) we were as alike as eggs. But when we were hatched and feathered it became suddenly evident that each of us was covered with a different plumage. Then as our wings grew we flew in the direction that had the greatest individual appeal. The difference in our creative power and our aspirations is not to be deplored; quite the contrary, it is an excellent sign. It should be so when the artistic individuality is maturing and gaining strength, which Balakirev never did and still does not understand.

In this differentiation of the members of the "mighty band" those who approached closest to the Conservatory and the taste of the general public attained greater success. At that time Chaikovsky was the favorite composer, and because of the brilliance of his orchestration Rimsky-Korsakov inherited this popularity. Borodin remained a "gentleman dilettante," known to only a chosen few; but he was indifferent to fame and was willing to wait calmly for posterity to pass its judgment upon him (which took place rather soon, for he died in 1887). The most tragic fate of all was that of Musorgsky, the greatest of the "mighty band," because he chose to remain loyal to his standard without making any concessions. In a letter dated 1872 he announced to Stasov his motto: "To the new shores," while as early as 1861, in answer to a querulous note of Balakirev, he wrote: "It is time to stop treating me as a child who needs to be put in swaddling clothes in order to prevent a fall."

What were "the new shores" that Musorgsky was anxious to reach? He disapproved of composers who followed rules imposed by the official routine. "This is not what the modern man demands of art, neither is it the artist's aim. Life, no matter where it finds expression; truth, no matter how bitter it be; fearlessness and words of sincerity to the people . . . that is my bent . . . that is what I want."

Thus men who were but recently friends went their different ways, and from that time on Musorgsky felt lonely, abandoned by everybody, and more and more often sought consolation in drink. With it all he continued to seek new ideas and was more fearless even than before, but his friends, including Stasov, unable any longer to understand him, predicted his downfall, and so left him to his fate. Musorgsky was forgotten in Russia, but when his aspirations, misunderstood during his lifetime, began to correspond to those of the new generation he was reborn to fame abroad. It was just at this period that Russia began to exert an influence on Europe, though it did not take place immediately. Before learning to appreciate Musorgsky in his original form foreigners came to know his music as interpreted by Rimsky-Korsakov, who rearranged all Musorgsky's unfinished works. *Khovanshchina* was the first one he finished (1881–82). Its impression on Rimsky-Korsakov was so fresh that he was able to reproduce the late composer's original ideas, but in order to adapt the opera for production he had to omit half the collected material. He proceeded with the task cautiously and with great tact, adding almost nothing of his own and merging his work into the personality of his late friend. *Boris Godunov,* the opera which needed only a finishing touch, was rearranged twenty years later (1896). But by that time Rimsky-Korsakov had changed, for he had studied Wagner's scores and had adopted his method of orchestration. When the West protested against Wagner this protest was reflected in Russia and led to the immediate revaluation of the works of Rimsky-Korsakov and Musorgsky. Rimsky-Korsakov's brilliant rearrangement of *Boris Godunov,* which had already been produced everywhere in Europe, suddenly appeared too much like Wagner. The new admirers then sought the original Musorgsky, and to their astonishment and delight, found him in his songs and piano compositions.

It would be unfair, indeed, to ascribe the new period in the history of Russian music, which then acquired world importance, exclusively to Musorgsky. Besides Rubinstein and Chaikovsky, the two composers of the so-called "cosmopolitan school," who had preceded Musorgsky in popularity abroad, Borodin too became known in Europe at first mostly for his quartets, which continued to grow in favor, and exerted a definite influence on the music of Debussy and Ravel. The combination of Borodin's polyphonic style and his most original melodies suited perfectly the new trend in music. Nevertheless Musorgsky's success in the West was far greater. As early as 1896–1900 Pierre d'Alheim and his wife, the singer Olenina-d'Alheim, had introduced his works in France and Belgium. Debussy had the chance to study the piano score of *Boris Godunov,* brought by Saint-Saens from Russia in 1879, but it was Musorgsky's songs that made a lasting impression upon him. In 1900–06 Olenina-d'Alheim carried Musorgsky's songs back to Russia, and this time the forgotten works of the prophet not without honor save in his own country earned the acclaim of his own people. Shaliapin's inspired interpretation of Musorgsky's music greatly assisted its success. After a long absence from the Imperial opera Rimsky-Korsakov's version of *Boris Godunov* was again produced in 1904 at the Mariinsky Theatre in St. Petersburg. *Khovanshchina,* which had been rejected in 1882, was produced in 1911. After that both operas were introduced in Paris and other European cities, and during the nineteen-twenties, with Borodin's *Prince Igor,* became renowned the world over. Thus, after a period of twenty years, the creative genius of Musorgsky led Russia to the modern music of the twentieth century.

Vladimir Rebikov (1866–1920), the first "Decadent" in Russian music, survived the revolution, but has long since been forgotten and surpassed. Some of his modern ideas he acquired in Germany where he had studied at the end of the nineteenth century. Rebikov's sympathy with the modern literary trends in Russia is expressed in his being the first to adapt the verses of Balmont and Briusov [7] to his musical sketches. He was also one of the first to abandon the massive musical compositions of masters of harmony and to compose musical miniatures. From the standpoint of technique this was a liberation from traditional form and

[7] On Balmont and Briusov, the two leading poets of the Symbolist school in Russia, see Part II, ch. 3.—ED.

harmony. Rebikov thought music a "language of emotions, and emotions possess no form, laws, or rules." As a true and conscientious Impressionist, he declared anything was permissible in harmony, and so employed most unusual chords. He ended his miniatures abruptly on a dissonant chord instead of the tonic, emphasizing thereby the fleeting impression of a psychological moment. Although after the beginning of the twentieth century Rebikov began to lag behind the other composers, he was fairly justified in regarding both Skriabin and Debussy as his imitators.

Before proceeding any further we must stop to examine the attitude of some other Russian musicians towards these new ideas. It was that of opposition, and the center of this opposition was the Moscow Conservatory, where Chaikovsky ruled supreme. During the struggle against modern methods introduced from the West in the era of Wagner and his followers, Brahms was the Muscovites' latest ideal, and S. Taneiev (1856–1915), the best of Chaikovsky's pupils, was called the "Russian Brahms." He sought the secrets of harmony in the old "strict style" of the thirteenth- and fifteenth-century contrapuntists. Like Brahms, Taneiev, also a recluse, looked for beauty in music and found it in a sentiment solemn and profound. His works, like those of Brahms, are not easy to understand, and their beauty is not fully revealed until one studies them closely. Indeed, both Brahms and Taneiev possessed a modern note, but in their conceptions they strictly adhered to Beethoven's classicism; they both regarded Wagner, and even more so the further development of music, as deviating sadly from the straight road. Taneiev lived long enough to see the great changes in the psychology of music, but he remained a stranger to them all and only retired the more into himself. However, his works were beyond the changing fashions, and consequently outlived them.

Others in Moscow were not satisfied with remaining passive, and so when Skriabin appeared on the scene the Conservatory organized an active opposition to the influence he was exerting. Rakhmaninov (b. 1873), a pupil of Taneiev and follower of Chaikovsky, led this movement in an effort to protect the old tradition from modernism. He was a native of Moscow and not altogether a stranger to new ideas. But as the years went by he became rather

pessimistic, and he developed a lyric strain even more intense
than that of Chaikovsky. During the period of dry and artificial
objectivity in music such lyricism appeared an anachronism, and
for a time the representatives of the modern trends forced Rakhmaninov into the background, virtually ignoring him. But he
became famous as an exceptionally talented pianist acclaimed
throughout the world, as are his brilliant compositions.

Medtner (b. 1879), a Russianized German, composed music
which reminds one more of Brahms than Chaikovsky and is understood only by a select few. He never aspired to fame and was
content with his own ideas. Although he opposed innovators of
Skriabin's type, Medtner nevertheless promoted the modern German influences. As a philosopher in music he sought the themes for
his songs in the works of Nietzsche, Tiutchev, and Andrey Bely,[8]
and thought that the "three great B's" (Bach, Beethoven, and
Brahms) were his forerunners. Instead of the confused rhythm of
the Impressionists, Medtner uses the clear rhythm of the classics,
although complicated somewhat by those of Schumann and
Brahms, and instead of the intricate modern harmony a rather
dry polyphonic form. In 1905 when the Brahms Society was
formed in Moscow, Medtner was surrounded by a group of enthusiastic admirers, but with the emigration his popularity has
unjustly decreased.

The true innovators took their origin in St. Petersburg, where
at their initial stage they were connected with the World of Art.[9]
The new ideas embodied in Russian music and art were introduced
by Diagilev to Europe, where, after their first great success, they
continued to develop in the latest European manner, and followed
all its many changes. In this process it is possible to trace the succession of stages closely corresponding to those in the development
of Western music. Impressionism was replaced with extreme forms
of Expressionism, followed by a return to a "pure" form, which led
to the revival of the polyphonic and pre-polyphonic periods, and
finally all radical tendencies were abandoned in favor of methods
and styles that shortly before had been regarded as being absolutely

[8] F. Tiutchev (1803–73), Russian poet known for the philosophical trend of his
poetry. On Andrey Bely, one of the Russian Symbolists, see Part II, ch. 3.—ED.
[9] See above, ch. 3.—ED.

antiquated. We see in these quests of the new generation the same inconclusiveness as in other branches of art, and the same search for new and unknown styles to replace the outmoded ones.

The historian's study of these parallel stages in modern European and Russian music is greatly facilitated by the fact that Igor Stravinsky passed through all of them and in the process was transformed gradually from a composer representative of a definite epoch in Russian music into a leader recognized by all Europe.

Stravinsky (b. 1886) took private lessons in composition from Rimsky-Korsakov, whom he met in 1902 at Heidelberg, and his first works up to 1908 were influenced by the atmosphere that prevailed at the St. Petersburg Conservatory. Notwithstanding some early signs of modern tendencies Stravinsky until 1911 did not break the artistic ties which united him with the style represented in Russia by Rimsky-Korsakov; he only introduced characteristics peculiar to the Russian "decadent" aestheticism of those years, which, however, were not irreconcilable with the style of Rimsky-Korsakov's latest period. Rimsky-Korsakov had already effected the transition from romanticism to fantastic fairy tales, treated lightly and with humor, so that musical aestheticism had only to emphasize the element of unreality and to lend a note of burlesque to his humor. Stravinsky's admirers stress the objectivity of his style, which they connect with the return to "pure" music. However, one hesitates to call "pure" music the works of Stravinsky composed for Diagilev's Ballet Russe, because in spite of his wish to remain independent in *L'Oiseau de feu* he was limited by Fokin's scenario, in *Petrushka* by Benois' conception of that production, and in *Le Sacre du printemps* by Roerich's stylization. In each of these works his music obediently follows the plot. Like the Impressionists, Stravinsky expresses himself "by means of color rather than line," but it is exactly in this that his connection with Rimsky-Korsakov's orchestration is most evident. Of course, in his use of the timbre of various instruments Stravinsky is more advanced than Rimsky-Korsakov, but in the development of harmonic nuances he follows along the same lines. All his early work is still connected with the harmonic period, which in Russia and in the West was nearing its final stage. In music, as in painting, Impressionism developed rather imperceptibly from Russian realism, and equally, as in painting, it found its expression in the increase of dynamics and in an ever progressing simplification and disfigurement of traditional forms, until it reached the stage of Expressionism. In 1908–11 we can see the beginning of that new process, which is already familiar to us through the history of painting.

In Europe the period of "stripping" music was connected with the name of the Expressionist Schoenberg. But for the Russia of those days Schoenberg was too extravagant and difficult to understand, so that his influence passed almost unnoticed. The ties with French Impressionism were much closer, because Debussy, who himself had come under the influence of Borodin and Musorgsky, had visited Russia and had left his mark on the work of modern Russian composers. It is very difficult to trace the transition from Debussy to Schoenberg, from Impressionism to Expressionism, in Russian music. Karatygin (1875–1925), the musical critic, who was an unprejudiced witness of that period, met Schoenberg when the latter came to Russia in 1912. The critic was ready to acknowledge Schoenberg's genius, but he declined to understand the logic of his methods, and though he felt that "here Impressionism had reached its limits," he was unable to supply any other definition, and this fact worried and annoyed him. Karatygin connected Schoenberg's name with that of Stravinsky: "Stravinsky, like Schoenberg, the German modernist, has reached the extreme limit in the refinement of tone. I wonder whether it will be with the names of Schoenberg and Stravinsky that the course of Impressionist development in European music will end?" This was written in 1914 in connection with the production of *Le Sacre du printemps*. But as early as 1912 Karatygin told of Schoenberg's works gaining popularity in Russia.

The pronounced and convinced modernists provoke laughter and hisses from the audience. So it was with Schoenberg both in Europe and Russia. . . . In St. Petersburg a year ago [i. e., 1911], at the "Nights of Contemporary Music," when Schoenberg's Opus Eleven for the piano [Expressionist, composed in 1909] was introduced to the public it was received with roars of laughter. Recently . . . the wonderful Opus Ten of Schoenberg's first period (1906) was performed and met with far fewer objections. . . . But yesterday, at the per-

formance of his *Pélléas et Mélisande,* a symphonic poem (composed
in his early manner of 1902) there were no hisses, but actually some
applause.

While exposing the shortcomings of the composer, Karatygin at
the same time emphasized "the great talent felt in every single
measure, in the wealth of thematic inventiveness, in his firm, bold
harmony, and in his exceptional mastery of ornamental polyphony.
. . . Schoenberg is laconic, profoundly original, madly bold, but
he has also an iron logic." It is important for us to note that on
December 13/26, 1912, in reference to this review, Stravinsky
wrote Karatygin the following lines from Clarens, where he was
finishing his *Sacre du printemps:*

I realize from what you write that you admire and understand what
is inherent in Schoenberg, this truly remarkable artist of our time.
Therefore I think that you would be interested in his latest work,
where his creative power finds its noblest expression. I speak of
*Dreimal Sieben Gedichte aus Albert Giraud's "Lieder des Pierrot
Lunaire" für eine Sprechstimme, Klavier, Floete (auch Piccolo),
Klarinette (auch Bassklarinette), Violine (auch Alto) und Violon-
celle.* It is what you, the "Contemporaries," ought to play. But perhaps you have already met him and he has told you about it, as he
told me.

Having learned the facts about Schoenberg's personal influence
and the high esteem in which Karatygin and Stravinsky held him,
we can return to the characterization of Stravinsky's work during
the new period, which began subsequent to 1911.

The large audience which in 1913 protested violently against the
music of *Le Sacre du printemps,* when it was introduced in the
regular season of the Ballet Russe, nevertheless felt instinctively
that it was a new and unusual step in the development of music.
The very choice of the subject was significant. From playing at
"barbarism" in *L'Oiseau de feu,* which in 1910 had pleased the
French public, and from burlesque *Petrushka* of 1911, Stravinsky
the composer, following the example of Roerich the painter, passed
to an attempt at reproducing a genuine prehistoric primitive, not
only barbaric, but even savage. And in order to achieve that
he had to introduce new colors into his music. Without attaining

the polytonality and atonality, the polyrhythms and arhythms of Schoenberg and his disciples, Stravinsky nevertheless, in his experiments in harmony and rhythm, made great progress in that direction.

The new period in the development of Western music represented a return to melody from the exclusive domination by harmony characteristic of the nineteenth century. Although Stravinsky's strength lay in harmony and rhythm, while his melodic inventiveness was not outstanding, the new stage in the development of his music was unanimously described by the critics as one of transition from the vertical harmonic style to the linear melodic one.

It was then that Impressionism, as seen in the works of Rimsky-Korsakov, and the aestheticism of the end of the century were both abandoned. True, Stravinsky retained his rôle of illustrator of the everchanging, picturesque moments in composing *Le Rossignol,* which was begun in 1909 and finished in 1914, in time for the Ballet Russe season, and in which he made his orchestra display all the iridescent shades and timbres possible. But B. F. Schloezer was correct in saying that *Le Rossignol* should be considered the first work in the "melodic period" of Stravinsky's art, and that it "represented a phase in which the composer collected his thoughts and hesitated between the two opposite issues open to him—the play of sounds and the prevalence of melody." In the meantime Stravinsky was transformed from a Russian into a European composer. He complied with the change in public taste, and the "Orient" in *Le Rossignol* ceased to be Russian or Asiatic and became pseudo-Chinese. But soon all exoticism disappeared from Stravinsky's music. Simultaneously with Diagilev's Ballet Russe, Stravinsky was definitely Europeanized and before long exercised a marked influence over the young French composers. In order to attain this position it was necessary for him to speak the new Western language of music, and so Stravinsky directed his creative power along these lines. It must not be forgotten that during this period—1914-19—"intellect was more important than inspiration."

With the strengthening of the intellectual element that of experimentation also increased in power, and with it Stravinsky's music became actually "pure," in the sense that he sought new effects in the surprising combinations of sound and timbre. In following the general trend of modern music which, by that time, had been established in the West, Stravinsky began to use chiefly instruments with a clear, distinct timbre, far removed from the modulations of the human voice or of stringed instruments. Thus in trying to create a new style Stravinsky, like his foreign colleagues, used an orchestra of unusual type in which the combination of instruments was changed to accord with the nature of the experiment. All this, of course, was reflected in the productions of the Ballet Russe, although this time it was not Stravinsky who served Diagilev's purposes, but Diagilev those of Stravinsky. *The Little Fox* (season of 1922) and *Wedding Feast* (season of 1923, composed in 1914–18) introduced a change in the style of music and in the character of the Ballet Russe.

Finally, in 1919 Stravinsky once again sought new and different ideas and methods, and both critics and loyal admirers found it very difficult to follow his strenuous efforts to grasp the modern movements and to satisfy the new taste.

This taste demanded that the old masters of the polyphonic, that is pre-classic, period be resuscitated. Diagilev had just found in the library at Milan a manuscript by Pergolesi, the composer of *Serva-Padrona* (1710–36) and father of *opéra bouffe*. It was exactly what was needed for the Russian Ballet, and he suggested to Stravinsky that he arrange the pieces of manuscript into a ballet. Stravinsky accepted the offer but instead of an ordinary arrangement he composed *Pulcinella* (season 1920), an original creation, in which, however, he preserved the spirit of the light and witty Neapolitan sketch and refrained from extreme modern harmonies. The return to Italian was followed by a return to Russian style. *Mavra,* a comic opera, was composed by Diagilev's order for the season of 1922 and was dedicated to Glinka, Chaikovsky, and Pushkin. In this work, with its syncopated American rhythms, frequent modulations, retarded cadences, and absence of the string quartet from the orchestra, Stravinsky was equally far removed from his prototypes. Yet he nevertheless sustained the key, introduced *bel canto,* and even deigned to adopt melodies from Russian, Gypsy, and Italian sources. Thus it justified the motto "Return to classicism," while the irony that permeated *Mavra* protected the

composer from being accused of apostasy. However, he ostenta-
tiously displayed his return to classicism in his *Apollon Musagète*
and *King Oedipus* (both composed in 1927), his return to Bach
in a piano concèrto (1924), and again to Chaikovsky in *The Kiss
of a Fairy*. Each of these works confused the public and critics
with its new method of composition. The orchestra grew ever
smaller (in *King Oedipus* Stravinsky resorted to strings only), the
harmony became more simple, the style more and more translu-
cent, and dynamics yielded to majestic immobility. "It is only left
for him to compose a mass," remarked Schloezer after *King Oedipus,* but instead Stravinsky astonished the public once again by
composing *The Kiss of a Fairy*. When finally he arrived at the
conception of a religious subject he produced the *Symphony of
Psalms* (1930). In this work Stravinsky wiped out entirely his
many experiments and returned to the colorful orchestration of
which he was such a great master during his early creative period.
The result was immediate: the public received the symphony with
tremendous enthusiasm, while the critics found themselves in an
awkward position, wondering "where Stravinsky was directing
his gaze."

Another great name in Russian and in contemporary music
generally, is that of Prokofiev. He is not only ten years younger
than Stravinsky but by nature is a different and in many respects
even a contradictory type. What Stravinsky attained with long
study and close work on the score, came to Prokofiev as a gift.
Everyone applies the words "young" and "cheerful" to him, the
critics say that he "sings like a bird," and the opinion is unanimous
that this young composer's creative power is inexhaustible. In
his spontaneity, naïveté, eternal youth, and great productivity
Prokofiev resembles Haydn and Mozart. While Stravinsky's meta-
morphoses were many and painful, Prokofiev's works are uniform
in their precipitous flow, and the critics, whose opinion of Stravinsky was ever in sharp disagreement, are unanimous about Prokofiev. Only towards the end of his evolution did Stravinsky
return to classicism, whereas Prokofiev, in a sense, is a classicist
by nature—a classicist from the very beginning, notwithstanding
the fancies and whims that outwardly express his buoyant imagination, and the spontaneous manner in which he welcomes every

new fashion. This is because he cannot give up his individuality; reflection and *Gruebelei* are alien to his nature. His youthful arrogance and innocent desire to cause astonishment should be attributed to this and not to snobbishness. Prokofiev was the appropriate person to protest against every type of psychology, philosophy, metaphysics, and mysticism in music, and, fortunately for him, he appeared when the time was ripe for this protest (approximately in 1909–11).

In what does Prokofiev's "classicism" consist? To begin with, in refusing to divide the timbres of various groups of instruments in the orchestra for colorful effects, and in acceptance of the orchestra as a whole. For as such it is more adaptable to the unfolding of themes in the classic cyclic form than to creating of romantic moods by spreading the melody over a harmonious background of soft and voluptuous chords. Instead of being colorful, Prokofiev's orchestra is graphic, and because of his individual peculiarities it is also brusque and pungent. This allows of sharp contrasts, abrupt turns, and the revival of melody, which scientific music had such difficulty in achieving, and which Prokofiev uses with such inexhaustible inventiveness. Rhythms are clear and accurate, which makes his music simple to understand and fascinates the audience. Prokofiev's art is not for the chosen few; it brings music back to the concert halls and thus makes it accessible to the masses.

Indeed, all these characteristics are not mere reminiscences of the classic epoch, for Prokofiev is modern, wanting to live the life of his time—and to its full extent. He adopts the dynamic spirit of the day with its impetuous, "cinematographic" aspect. His buoyancy is healthy and contagious, while he unfolds themes with such originality and lack of repetition that the audience has no time in which to relax.

Although Prokofiev is not an advocate of "pure" music he is actually serving it. He need not assume an attitude of protest against the literary and philosophic influences in music, because this position was assured before he appeared, but he profited nevertheless by the fruits of that conquest and paid his tribute to the times by choosing comic subjects for his compositions for the operatic stage.

What place does Prokofiev occupy in modern music's scheme of evolution analogous to that in the development of painting? We have called him a "classicist"—a term generally accepted as the opposite of "romanticist." But Prokofiev's buoyant temperament makes it rather difficult to assign him a definite place within the limits of any scheme. However, it is not only possible but quite natural to draw a parallel between his music and the corresponding moment in the history of painting. This gives us also the opportunity of filling the gap between Expressionism and the return to the past, which was left open when speaking of Stravinsky's evolution. We know that in painting there was not only a negative protest against the lack of form in Impressionism but also a positive effort to replace it with correct drawing and definite form. Prokofiev's art represents a similar stage in the development of Russian music. In an article published in *Rech* during 1916 Karatygin likened Prokofiev to the most sincere and talented of the Russian Cubist and Futurist artists. And in fact this parallel is fully justified by Prokofiev's outstanding characteristic—the return from the shapeless and colorful Neo-Impressionism to a definite form.

The youngest generation of modern Russian composers grew up under the influence of Stravinsky and Prokofiev, but they began working independently at a time when even their masters regarded the changes which took place during the first twenty years of the twentieth century as a matter of the past. Thus, being able to profit not only by the experience of their immediate predecessors, but also by that of the leaders of the preceding "harmonic" and "classic" periods, this young generation developed a broader outlook on the problems and methods of modern music. But of course in all their works the influence of Stravinsky and Prokofiev is particularly marked. We shall now cite as examples the names of a few young composers who have gained renown in the world of music. Markevich, even in his recent emancipation from the extremes of modern music, is a foremost follower of Stravinsky. Nabokov, a disciple of Prokofiev, like his master possesses an enthusiasm for modernistic music, temperament, and a spontaneous inspiration. The youngest of this generation, Julius Krein, the son of Alexander Krein, shows independence from both Stravinsky and Prokofiev and follows—in so far as he follows anyone—the

older romanticists and classicists of music. Of course, the ways of
these young musicians are barely marked at present, and only the
future can define their true character.

Music presents a tragic picture of ruins in post-revolutionary
Russia. With great difficulty some young shoots are making their
appearance from this chaos, but they are not "new" in the sense
of being in harmony with their modern surroundings. To some
extent the reasons for this chaos in music were the same as in
literature. In both fields the most outstanding representatives of
the pre-revolutionary period had emigrated abroad. Stravinsky was
already at home in Western Europe when he was joined there by
Rakhmaninov, Grechaninov, Medtner, and temporarily by Prokofiev. Talented conductors, singers, pianists, violinists, and 'cel-
lists soon found work abroad. Those who remained in Russia were
forced to lead a life of privation and dire need. With the institution of the NEP (New Economic Policy) artistic as well as all
other enterprises were declared self-supporting, and another difficulty presented itself. There was no audience sufficiently educated
to appreciate the subtleties of ultra-modernistic music; serious concerts did not pay expenses, and all the new compositions of this
type were therefore destined to be heard only by a small circle of
intimate friends, with no hope of ever being published; as to the
larger and more important forms of composition, they could not
even be publicly performed. It became more and more difficult
to form an orchestra because, while many musicians played
stringed instruments, very few could play the wind instruments.
The young musicians were not interested in the oboe, flute, and
brasses, and the older ones were gradually dying out. Moreover,
the democratic spirit of the musicians found expression in a protest against the conductor's right to restrict the freedom of the
members of the orchestra, and in 1922 they formed a conductorless
orchestra (the First Symphony Ensemble, or *Persimfans*). As long
as they retained their original enthusiasm and were playing familiar pieces this enterprise was successful, but when it came to
learning new music, both the will and discipline vanished.

The destruction of the young shoots was due chiefly to the
opposition between the social command ordering modern music
for the masses, and the production, which adhered steadfastly to

the methods of the recent past. These methods had satisfied the
refined and decadent taste of the Moscow Maecenases who patronized any new combination of words, color, and sound. Thus, as
these works were only for the benefit of the chosen few, the rough,
uncultured masses could not appreciate them, and unfortunately
there was no one able to restore health to the decadent art. At
first, during the period of War Communism, efforts were made
to cultivate the very latest in music, thinking it (as in art it was
thought of the Futurists) the most revolutionary. In this spirit
A. S. Lurie tried to "command" the affairs of music. But soon it
was realized that music of the modern type had no public, and
that the present one needed something more simple, rhythmical,
melodious, and gay. Besides the social command there was also
a governmental command ordering propaganda music to be composed for solemn occasions. Contributors of course were found,
but curiously enough they either represented that most conservative type of music, the church chant, or else were those who under the old régime composed cantatas for coronations, triumphal
marches, and festival music. No wonder that the true musicians
retired into themselves and, deaf to the new call, continued to work
along the old lines, although with slight modifications.

To some extent we know these tendencies. In fact, revolution
did not find any single trend dominating music, for it was really
the period when all sought new ideas and bore the banner of innovators. The actual quality of their aspirations is better expressed
by what was repudiated than by that which attracted them. They
repudiated the opera, a form of music most appreciated by the
general public. Opera was condemned as an artificial, conventional,
and mixed form of music, not meeting the requirements of either
realistic art or free inspiration. Even before the revolution the
young composers showed preference for symphonic and chamber music, and after the October Revolution this tendency was
strengthened by the fact that in both capitals the state opera remained under the old administration, which was averse to patronizing innovators and preferred modern staging of old operas such
as *Faust* and *Carmen*. It was quite useless to compose music obviously destined to remain in the composer's portfolio; moreover,
operas with a national spirit were considered outmoded, and new

themes, within the comprehension of the masses, were difficult
to find.

At the same time the grandiose, monumental, and heroic themes
suggested by the extraordinary events of the day did not appeal
to the composers. Revolution had not yet had time to be covered
with the growth of poetry and legend; and it was not so easy for
a learned composer to sing of it in its crude state in music, as it
was for a self-taught author in literature. Ideas on a grand scale,
in Skriabin's style, also lost their attraction, for, apart from the
fact that to carry them out required Skriabin's naïve conceit, mysticism at that time was out of place. Sabaneiev gives an excellent
description of the desire to "de-skriabinize" Soviet music:

We were convinced that nothing ages as quickly as "novelty," and
that there is nothing older than yesterday's novelty. . . . After
Skriabin's subtleties, after his mystic ecstasies . . . we longed to
cultivate lapidary, rather coarse, comic and grotesque moods. We
required something fresh, vivid, lifelike, and cheerful in exchange
for that overstrained, ecstatic, very fascinating, but nevertheless un-
healthy atmosphere. There was no fresh air in Skriabin's works,
only the ecstasy produced by an opiate, leading to the world of
hallucinations.

The new slogan was "Back to health." In literature this same
mood was expressed by a return to artistic realism,[10] but in music
it was more complicated. "The natural course," Sabaneiev continues, "led to the enemy camp of musical academism." But the
innovators did not believe in this course, and we see them in a
state of confusion unable to form any definite ideas, although at
times it is possible to detect the existence of some great creative
impulses. This explains the pronounced failure of the Soviet composers to devote themselves to revolutionary themes, their absten-
tion from definite utterings, and their intentional vagueness.
Among creative musicians in Soviet Russia Sabaneiev places at
the head of the list the following three names: N. Miaskovsky,
S. Feinberg, and Anatole Aleksandrov. As they are little known
abroad we shall adhere to the characterizations as given by Sabaneiev, who with N. Roslavets had represented the most radical

[10] See Part II, chs. 4 and 5.—ED.

trend in Soviet music. Miaskovsky (b. 1881), a pupil of Glazunov and Rimsky-Korsakov, has composed many symphonies, and although a classmate of Prokofiev at the Conservatory, their temperaments are as opposite as the poles. Miaskovsky is so extremely melancholy and distressingly troubled that it makes his music somber and vague.[11] His manner of composition is restrained. His music is serious and a masterpiece of technique, but it has no outstanding individuality and tends to preserve a balance between modernism and conservatism. He is related to Chaikovsky through his lyrical pessimism and melancholy. However, he is also subject to other influences, ranging from Mozart and Grieg to Debussy and Skriabin, which makes him so changeable that his compositions lack individual style.

Feinberg (b. 1889), a pianist and composer for the piano, is in music a visionary forever surrounded by phantoms. His compositions somewhat resemble Skriabin, but without the latter's "Titanic pose," while his sonatas in many respects remind one of Schumann. Feinberg is a mystic and a belated romanticist, who continues to seek harmonies beyond the earthly reach. He composes only for himself, and his seven sonatas, which are extremely difficult, are little known outside the circle of his most intimate friends.

Anatole Aleksandrov (b. 1889), a "typical retrospectivist and painstaking composer of musical miniatures," spiritually resembles Medtner. He of them all is "the least affected by the cosmic influence of the revolution"; he is "imperturbable in his academism which, however, is no longer based on the classical substrata of Brahms, but on the modern ones of Skriabin and Medtner."

Further on, Sabaneiev names three national Jewish composers, M. Gnesin and Alexander and Gregory Krein. Gnesin is cold and scientific in his approach to the creation of national Jewish music. He also tried to compose a "revolutionary" symphony to Sergey Esenin's words, but failed to attain in it the "monumental style" which the Bolsheviks exacted; this work is far more typical of one of Rimsky-Korsakov's pupils or a disciple of the national Russian school than of a revolutionary innovator. Neither does Gregory Krein's style of composition show much effect of the revolutionary

11 Cf. the editor's remarks on this subject in his postscript to this volume.—Ed.

years, and it is only Alexander Krein who is rather inclined "to leave the intimate circle and venture forth into a wider field," for in contrast to Gnesin he is passionate and temperamental. Although, like Rebikov, he repudiates the musical tradition in a revolutionary manner, he remains profoundly national. In him flows the Oriental blood of the race by which the *Song of Songs* was created, and from Ravel and Debussy he turns to the melodies of the ancient synagogue, which he endows with all the dynamic of his emotional nature. He is too realistic to be satisfied with Neo-Impressionism.

As we see, none of the outstanding composers who continued to work in the Soviet Union was the product of the October Revolution.[12] They were all born in the eighteen-eighties, and their creative power developed under the influences that prevailed at the border line of the two centuries. In those days radicalism in music was definitely artistic. The very nature of the extreme trends, which had as their aim the liberation of music from any literary, philosophic, or other similar association, rather alienated than connected the innovators with politics. This being the mood of the more gifted artists of Soviet Russia they could not possibly create the "monumental, heroic, and grandiose new revolutionary music" required of them by the Communist policy. But even in the field of music there soon appeared some followers of the radical trends, who, profiting by the play on words, established a connection with the radical political trends and tried to attain power under the new régime. Nicholas Roslavets (b. 1880), the Maiakovsky of music,[13] was the most outstanding among these "Fellow Travelers" and developed his own "formal" method. Having declared himself a "Positivist" and Marxist, Roslavets derided the "soul of music," and following a strictly "scientific formula" he composed "soulless, formalist music." But his theory, intended for a restricted circle of "connoisseurs of the perfect form," was as contrary to the Soviet slogan "Bring music to the masses" as was that of the Formalists in literature.[14] The workmen's clubs needed quite a different music, and when composing "revolutionary

12 Cf. the editor's postscript to this volume.—ED.
13 On Maiakovsky, the Futurist poet of Soviet Russia, see Part II, ch. 4.—ED.
14 See Part II, ch. 4.—ED.

works" even Roslavets was obliged to simplify his musical language. His rivals declared that "in his cantata *October* Roslavets defeated himself by repudiating all his previous compositions." This composer was to share the fate of the literary Formalists.

Boleslav Iavorsky, another alchemist in music, was far more fortunate, for he succeeded in making obligatory, at all the schools where he taught, the study of his theory in which he gave his explanation of harmony. For some time the number of his pupils was so great that all the students of music were divided into two cliques—"Iavorskists" and "Anti-Iavorskists." While Iavorsky could produce no examples to prove the superiority of his theory, his pupils, of whom Melkikh and Protopopov were the most outstanding, were rendered powerless by the thousand and one trivial rules of this esoteric teaching. In the mean time, the urgent command was issued for music to be of easy access to the masses, and it was necessary to accelerate the production of simple compositions. At this juncture the anxiety of the authorities was relieved by the composers of minor importance, who had been trained under the old régime, but were able to adapt themselves to the new requirements. A. Ostretsov, in a review of 1928, remarks that "such composers as G. Lobachev, D. Vasiliev-Buglay, and K. Korchmarev, were the first to answer the needs of the masses and actually showed how and along what lines the work had to be done." These representatives of the "labor trend" waged war on "aestheticism of the Impressionist type and on the art of pure, self-sufficient forms." For "choral collectives" Lobachev composed "precise and graphic pieces with a firm and bold rhythmical step, ending in fiery trumpet fanfares," on the themes *Mutiny Call, Victory Song, Form into Ranks,* and the like. Korchmarev, though outwardly connected with Rimsky-Korsakov's tradition, aspired nevertheless to "intensify the exhibition of man's social attitude towards reality," and so composed such characteristic pieces as *Engine C 15* and *Komsomol Leap Frog.* The reviewer admits, however, that "the sovietization of the Fellow Travelers was a process infinitely complicated and difficult. The charms of Debussy still exert great power over their mind, and the fact that Lobachev, and particularly Korchmarev, are attracted by French music is not to be denied." The example of Arthur Lurie, a "Decadent" and "Neo-Impressionist," who had been the Commissar for Music and a dictator in that field, but later escaped to Paris, proves that it was almost impossible to rely upon these older men. The same reservations may be applied to Zolotarev (b. 1873), a pupil of Rimsky-Korsakov, Gliere, Ippolitov-Ivanov, and others. The Communists hold out more hope of the young generation of composers, which "follows an experimental course and submits its works to tests on the stage of workmen's clubs."

Undoubtedly the social upheaval, which brought the lower and upper strata closer together, also supplied new opportunities to music such as it had never had at the time of the aesthetic salons. The working masses were no longer satisfied with their old *chastushka* (a musical limerick) and demanded new music.

The dearth of suitable new music makes it necessary to choose from that of the old repertory. The Soviet radio has recourse even to transmitting musical programs from foreign stations. Naturally all this will inevitably influence the coming generation of Russian composers in their choice of trends. What course will they take? In part Prokofiev's popularity in Soviet Russia gives us the answer. His music is cheerful, youthful, and easy to understand, and these are the properties demanded by the people.

EDITOR'S POSTSCRIPT

During the last decade it has been possible to observe in the field of Soviet architecture and painting a development closely similar to that which has been taking place in Soviet literature.[1] In both cases there has been a noticeable tendency to do away with the extremes of the earlier revolutionary period and to maintain a certain degree of ideological unity among the artists all of whom were expected to serve the same social purpose. Art, like literature, had to be sufficiently simple to be understood by the masses, and while it had to assimilate all the technical achievements of the past, it was not to lose sight of the final goal—the socialist reconstruction of society.

In architecture the starting point in recent development was the competition for the projected Palace of the Soviets in Moscow. In publishing its report on the award, the governmental commission in charge of the competition formulated the fundamental principles which, in the opinion of the authorities, should control Soviet architecture. It should be "a people's architecture, essentially humane and rich with details that should appeal to the masses." It should also be based on a careful study of the architectural styles of the past, thereby "gaining for the new all the benefits which the old had developed." The publication of the report was followed by a long and lively discussion among the architects themselves in which its general propositions were dealt with in a more detailed and specific fashion. The new governmental attitude, which the Soviet architects had to accept as a guiding principle, meant in the first place a rejection of such extremes as "Functionalism" and "Constructivism." The artistic content of architecture could not and should not be reduced to

[1] See the Editor's Postscript to Part II of this work.

the concept of the "function" of a given structure or to the forms
of the technique itself, because in both cases that would mean the
negation of architecture as an art. Of course, Soviet architects
should strive to create technically advanced and functionally adequate structures. But they should aim also at filling these structures with positive aesthetic content in harmony with the spirit
of the great historical epoch in which it was their privilege to live.

The governmental pronouncement meant further a condemnation of modernistic tendencies in architecture pursued for modernism's own sake. As in literature, the command was "to learn
from the classics." In the discussion that followed there was an
attempt to determine which of the past architectural styles were
more applicable to the problems of Soviet architecture. While it
was admitted that certain technical achievements could be borrowed from every one of these styles, the prevailing opinion
seemed to be that it was from the classical architecture of Greece
and Rome that one could learn most. All Oriental styles, as well as
Byzantine, Romanesque and Gothic, had been inspired by religion
and mysticism. And the last was also expressive of the feudal age,
just as the architecture of the Renaissance stood for the age of the
despots, and the "functional" style of the post-war period for that
of decadent capitalism. In contrast, classical architecture had been
essentially civic and social in inspiration, which made it a much
more acceptable model. Moreover, it had the advantage of offer-
ing a connecting link with the Empire style of the late eighteenth
and early nineteenth centuries in Russia, so that in following
the classics one could also keep up a national tradition.[2]

While the most outstanding works of Soviet architecture continued to be structures of a mass character, such as "palaces of
culture," workers' clubs and other public buildings, much more
attention has been paid during these last years to the construction of modern apartment houses, a fact that must be connected
with the new emphasis on the importance of family life and the
official proclamation of the era of good living to be enjoyed by all.

With regard to painting there was a similar condemnation
of extreme modernistic tendencies and of a formalist approach

[2] Cf. T. F. Hamlin, "Style Development in Soviet Architecture," *The American Quarterly of the Soviet Union*, Vol. I, No. 1 (1938).

emphasizing artistic technique at the expense of the ideological content of art. To painting was applied the same slogan of Socialist Realism which was made an obligatory theory for the Soviet writers. As in literary works, pictures had to reflect the heroic age of socialist construction with its struggles, victories and aspirations, and they had to do it in a way that would make them easily enjoyed and appreciated by the people at large, and not by a limited group of connoisseurs. In their effort to fulfil this task the Soviet painters began to devote themselves to representation of such subjects as episodes in the lives of revolutionary leaders (Stalin and Lenin in the first place), the civil war, work and play on collective farms, the Dnieprostroy power-plant, the ironworks at Magnitogorsk, the construction of the subway in Moscow, and the conquest of the Arctic.

As in literature, a certain amount of individual stylistic freedom was allowed, and some painters continued to preserve moderately modernistic tendencies while others adhered to the World of Art tradition. But in view of the official demands for an easily understandable and civic-minded art, it was inevitable that in most cases the Soviet painters should go beyond the World of Art to the realistic style of the Itinerants, which now experienced something like a posthumous rehabilitation.[3] And while official critics speak of "the inception of a new realistic art" in Soviet Russia, to an outside observer this art does not look particularly new in anything but subject matter. In its technique as well as in its general aesthetic approach it reproduces all the characteristic features of Russian painting as it was back in the 'seventies and 'eighties. We are faced here with the paradox of a revolutionary government sponsoring a highly conventional and definitely old-fashioned art.

Music by its very nature is less amenable to governmental regulation and ideological pressure from outside than either literature or arts. Perhaps this explains the fact, pointed out in the last chapter, that for a relatively long time many of the outstanding Soviet composers shunned revolutionary themes and tended to pursue each his own individual way. It has been noted, however, that towards the end of the preceding period a general demand

[3] On the World of Art and the Itinerants, see above, Ch. III.

was formulated for the Soviet composers to bring their art into harmony with the spirit of the time, and to satisfy the needs of the masses. The great success which awaited Prokofiev upon his return to Russia was due not only to his extraordinary talent, but also to the fact that his manly and cheerful music met with official approbation and was pointed out as an example to be followed. That this advice did not remain unheeded can be demonstrated best in the case of Miaskovsky. It appears that the characterization of his music as highly introspective and pessimistic is no longer applicable in view of the different nature of the works he has produced in the course of the last decade. Soviet commentators are unanimous in describing the evolution of Miaskovsky as one from "doubts and gloomy forebodings" to "optimism and faith." Quite obviously, the composer has made a conscientious effort to identify himself with the spirit of the time as his Twelfth Symphony (also known as the Kolkhoz or Collective Farm Symphony) was dedicated to the fifteenth anniversary of the October revolution, the Sixteenth to Soviet aviation, the Eighteenth to the twentieth anniversary of the revolution, and the Nineteenth to the Red Army, while in 1939 he wrote an overture to commemorate Stalin's sixtieth birthday. A somewhat similar tendency has been noticeable in the work of M. Shaporin (b. 1887) who in 1939 produced a symphonic cantata *On the Kulikovo Field,* which is "permeated with love for fatherland and freedom" and thus forms a musical counterpart to the recent "defense literature" in Soviet Russia. In all these works the critics find the same fundamental traits characteristic of most of Soviet music in its latest stage: a monumental style, the prevalence of major tonality, and a preference for martial rhythms.

The last decade saw also the emergence of younger Soviet composers whose musical growth did not start until after the revolution. Of these the most famous and, undoubtedly, the most gifted is D. Shostakovich (b. 1909). Having begun with a symphony which showed unmistakable affinity with pre-revolutionary Russian music, he then became affected by the influence of Western European musical modernists. In his opera *Lady Macbeth of Mtsensk,* however, he made an attempt to create a work with social content and, in his own words, "to make the music as simple and expressive as possible." Produced in 1934, the opera for a while enjoyed considerable success, but subsequently it was severely condemned as guilty both of "formalistic tendencies" and "vulgar naturalism," and its performance was discontinued by official order. The discussion which accompanied that act took the form of a veritable trial of Shostakovich who was accused of having fallen under the influence of such Western modernists as Schoenberg, Hindemith, Berg, and Křenek, representatives of the decadent bourgeois civilization and thus ideologically hostile to Soviet Russia. During the discussion Stalin was quoted to the effect that "music in Soviet Russia should be national in its form and socialist in content." Shostakovich remained in eclipse for two years, until the performance in January, 1938 of his Fifth Symphony which was acclaimed as a work of genius and led to his complete rehabilitation. In this symphony, according to the Soviet critics, Shostakovich has freed himself from all his former faults and has presented a work "glorifying the victory of a powerful personality over all doubts, and the joyous triumph of human reason." According to press reports, Shostakovich was engaged, on the eve of the present war, in writing his seventh symphony, with the image of Lenin as his inspiration.

Among the other younger composers one should mention A. Mosolov (b. 1900) whose *Iron Foundry,* in spite of its success abroad, has been condemned by Soviet critics for excessive modernism, but who in his Second Symphony (1934) has also "liberated himself of formalistic tendencies and has created a work emotionally satisfying and full of ideas"; I. Dzerzhinsky (b. 1909), author of the operas *Quiet Flows the Don* (1936) and *The Upturned Soil* (1937), with librettos based on Sholokhov's well-known novels; T. Khrennikov (b. 1913), whose First Symphony was performed in 1935, and A. Khachaturian (b. 1904). The last named, an Armenian by birth, is representative of the tendency on the part of many Soviet composers to achieve simplicity by turning to folklore, and together with others is responsible for the development of regional music in the Soviet Union (such as Armenian, Georgian, Bashkir, Turkoman, Uzbek, etc.). In the opinion of some writers the Oriental element in this regional music is much more authentic than that in the works of the pre-revolutionary "nationalist" school, but it remains to be seen whether such ethnographic transcription is more capable of great artistic achievement than the nostalgic longing of a Glinka, a Borodin or a Rimsky-Korsakov for the Orient of his dreams.

MICHAEL KARPOVICH

Cambridge, Mass.
October, 1941

BIBLIOGRAPHY

The purpose of this selected bibliography is to give suggestions for further reading on various topics treated in this volume. All else being equal, books in English have been given preference over those in other Western languages, and more recent works over the older ones. Articles in periodicals have been included only in those cases in which no adequate treatment in books was available. The apparent lack of balance between the separate sections of the bibliography is due to the fact that literature on certain periods and topics is more abundant than on others. Transliteration of Russian names has been left as it appears in the books and articles cited even when it differs from that used in the present volume.

CHAPTERS I–III

Ainalov, D. *Geschichte der russischen Monumentalkunst der vormoskovitischen Zeit.* Berlin and Leipzig, 1932.
—— *Geschichte der russischen Monumentalkunst zur Zeit des Grossfürstentums Moskau.* Berlin and Leipzig, 1933.
Alpatov, M. and Brunov, N. *Geschichte der altrussischen Kunst.* Two volumes. Baden bei Wien, 1932.
Volume I contains text, volume II illustrations.
L'Art byzantin chez les Slaves: l'ancienne Russie, les Slaves catholiques. Two volumes. Paris, 1932.
Benois, A. *The Russian School of Painting.* New York, 1916.
From the eighteenth century to the early twentieth century.
Buxton, D. *Russian Medieval Architecture.* New York, 1934.
Cross, S. and Conant, K. "The Earliest Medieval Churches of Kiev," *Speculum,* vol. XI (1936).
Farbman, M. (editor). *Masterpieces of Russian Painting.* London, 1930.
Reproductions of Russian icons and frescoes, with articles by various authors.
Hautecoeur, L. *L'Architecture classique à Saint-Pétersbourg à la fin du XVIIIᵉ siècle.* Paris, 1912.

Kondakov, N. *The Russian Icon*. Oxford, 1927.

Lieven, Prince P. *The Birth of Ballets-Russes*. Boston, 1936.

Muratov, P. *Les Icones russes*. Paris, 1927.

Newmarch, Rosa. *The Russian Arts*. New York, 1916.

Réau, Louis, *L'Art russe des origines à Pierre le Grand*. Paris, 1921.

—— *L'Art russe de Pierre le Grand à nos jours*. Paris, 1922.

—— and Loukomski, G. *Catherine la Grande, inspiratrice d'art et Mécène*. Paris, 1930

Rice, D. T. (editor). *Russian Art*. London, 1935.
Collection of articles by various authors.

Schweinfurth, P. *Geschichte der russischen Malerei im Mittelalter*. Hague, 1930.

Williams, H. *Russia of the Russians*. New York, 1915.
Chapter 9 deals with painting, chapter 10 with architecture.

Wulff, O. *Die neurussische Kunst: Im Rahmen der Kulturentwicklung Russlands von Peter den Grossen bis zur Revolution*. Two volumes. Baden bei Wien, 1932.
Volume I contains text, volume II illustrations.

—— and Alpatoff, M. *Denkmäler der Ikonenmalerei in Kunstgeschichtliher Folge bearbeitet*. Dresden, 1925.

CHAPTER IV

Beskin, O. *The Place of Art in the Soviet Union*. [The American Russian Institute for Cultural Relations with the Soviet Union, Special Publication No. 2]. New York, 1936.

Freeman, J., Kunitz, J. and Lozowick, L. *Voices of October: Art and Literature in Soviet Russia*. New York, 1930.
Contains "Soviet Painting and Architecture" by L. Lozowick.

Hamlin, T. F. "Style Development in Soviet Architecture," *The American Quarterly of the Soviet Union*, vol. I (1938).

Holme, C. G. (editor). *Art in the USSR*. London and New York, 1935.

London, Kurt. *The Seven Soviet Arts*. New Haven, 1938.
Part III contains sections on architecture and painting.

Painting, Sculpture and Graphic Art in the USSR. [VOKS Illustrated Almanac, 9–10]. Moscow, 1934.

CHAPTER V

Abraham, G. *Borodin: The Composer and His Music*. London, 1927.

—— *On Russian Music: Critical and Historical Studies*. New York, 1939.

—————— *Studies in Russian Music*. New York, 1936.
The last two volumes deal with the Russian "nationalist" school from Glinka to Glazunov.

Armitage, M. (editor). *Igor Stravinsky*. New York, 1936.
Collection of articles by various authors.

Bowen, Catherine D. *'Free Artist': The Story of Anton and Nicholas Rubinstein*. New York, 1939.

Calvocoressi, M. *Glinka: biographie critique*. Paris, n.d. [1911].

—————— and Abraham, G. *Masters of Russian Music*. New York, 1936.
From Glinka to Skriabin.

Evans, E. *Tchaikovsky*. London, 1935 [revised edition].

Freeman, J., and others. *Voices of October*. [See above, under Chapter IV].
Contains "Soviet Music" by J. Freeman.

Habets, A. *Borodin and Liszt*. London, 1895.
Based on Borodin's letters.

Hull, A. E. *A Great Russian Tone-Poet: Scriabin*. London, 1920 [2nd edition].

London, Kurt. *The Seven Soviet Arts*. [See above, under Chapter IV].
Part III, chapter 1 deals with music.

Montagu-Nathan, M. *A History of Russian Music*. London, 1918 [2nd edition].

—————— *Rimsky-Korsakof*. New York, 1917.

—————— *Contemporary Russian Composers*. New York, 1917.
The last volume deals with Skriabin, Glazunov, Stravinsky, Rachmaninov, Rebikov, Taneiev, Medtner, Cherepnin, Grechaninov, and "the younger generation."

Newmarch, Rosa. *The Russian Opera*. Now York, n.d. [1914].

Rachmaninoff's Recollections Told to Oscar von Riesemann. New York, 1934.

Riesemann, Oscar von. *Moussorgsky*. New York, 1929.

Rimsky-Korsakoff, N. *My Musical Life*. New York, 1923.

Sabaneyeff, L. *Modern Russian Composers*. New York, 1927.
From Taneiev to the early works of Soviet composers.

Schloezer, B. de. *Igor Stravinsky*. Paris, 1929.

Schneerson, G. "The Changing Course of Russian Music," *Modern Music,* vol. XIII, No. 2 (1936).

[Stravinsky, I.]. *Stravinsky: An Autobiography*. New York, 1936.

Tchaikovsky, M. *The Life and Letters of P. I. Tchaikovsky*. New York, 1906.

Vodarsky-Shiraeff, Alexandra. *Russian Composers and Musicians: A Biographical Dictionary*. New York, 1940.

Williams, H. *Russia of the Russians*. [See above, under Chapters I–III].

Chapter 7 deals with music.

INDEX